GW01066425

BIG SECRETS FROM BIG BROTHER

BIG SECRETS FROM BIG BROTHER

JULES STENSON
& LEWIS PANTHER

JB

JOHN BLAKE

Published by John Blake Publishing Ltd,
3 Bramber Court, 2 Bramber Road,
London W14 9PB, England

First published in Great Britain in paperback 2001

ISBN 1 903402 83 2

British Library Cataloguing-in-Publication Data:
A catalogue record for this book is available
from the British Library.

Typeset by Jon Davies

Printed in Great Britain by
Creative Print and Design (Wales), Ebbw Vale, Gwent

1 3 5 7 9 10 8 6 4 2

Contents

Acknowledgements

News of the World staff who have also helped create this book are:

Gary Thompson, Dave Jarvis, Paul Nicholas, Carole Aye Maung and David McGee.

Picture research by Clare Wood and Simon Lord.

Where no other source has been acknowledged, material in this book has been taken from Channel 4 and E4 broadcasts of *Big Brother II*, or from transcripts published on the Big Brother Web site.

Foreword

Foreword

On the morning of 25 May 2001, the unknown contestants for *Big Brother II* filed into the Channel 4 house in East London. Over the following weeks, they came out one by one — as household names.

Certainly they all hoped for celebrity — they wouldn't have applied to be on the show otherwise — but little could any of them have realised what a phenomenon the series would become. Or how it would change their lives.

It is easy to forget now the uncertainty that cloaked *BBII*. The first run of Big Brother had been the TV ratings success of summer 2000, and the following March a follow-up celebrity version in aid of Children in Need proved equally popular.

But was the public appetite now jaded? Channel 4's executives could certainly have been forgiven if they'd have felt a bit uneasy. The new *Big Brother* series was pitched against ITV's glossy ratings weapon, *Survivor*.

Already a huge hit in the United States, *Survivor* pitted rival contestants on a paradise island for the chance to win £1 million. Surely *Big Brother*, with its smaller prize of £70,000, could no longer compete, could it? You bet it could.

By the time Brian Dowling left the *Big Brother* house as the overall winner of series two, the programme had become a national obsession. Thousands of Brits enjoying summer breaks in Spain and Greece crowded around TV sets in any bar that could tune in to *Big Brother* on satellite feeds.

A staggering 4,230,000 viewers voted for Brian, with an impressive 2,680,000 more voting for his nearest rival, Helen Adams. Millions more watched enthralled as host Davina McCall fronted the final show.

How would Brian react to winning the £70,000? Would Helen and her favourite fellow housemate Paul finally find true romance?

This is the *uncensored* and *unauthorised* story of *Big Brother*, compiled with the help of contestants' friends and families.

In places, this book may shock you. Often, it will amuse you. But if, like the *News of the World*, you're a *Big Brother* fan, this book will fascinate you. Happy reading.

CHAPTER 1

HELEN & PAUL'S ROMANCE

'In the dream, Paul locked me in the bedroom ...
He told me, "You can't come out until you like me."
Well, I'll never come out then!'
HELEN ADAMS

Helen Adams screwed up her face as if she'd just tasted something particularly disgusting. 'If Paul Clarke came on to me, I think I'd be physically sick!' she shuddered.

And so began the romance that kept a nation hooked. The 'will they, won't they?' saga of Helen and Paul became one of the tabloid stories of the year.

Of course, as in many of the best love stories, no one would have predicted it after their first few weeks in the *Big Brother* house.

Helen thought that Paul was a 'lad'. Ladies' man Paul, though partial to blondes, thought Helen was dizzy, immature and, to put it bluntly, a pain in the arse! She got on his nerves so much that he even nominated her for eviction in the first vote. In fact, Helen was so scatter-brained in those early days she could well have been booted out after just two weeks — that is, if she hadn't been up against the even crazier Penny Ellis.

Just think if she had gone. There'd have been a minor fuss as Helen left the house, then she'd have gone back to her job at the Classy Cutz salon in Cwmbran, South Wales, and settled down with her boyfriend, Gavin 'Big G' Cox. Who knows, the pair may even have married.

Helen had made it perfectly clear

early on in the house that if Big G proposed she'd say 'Yes.' Mind you, she quickly went back on this rash pledge as her feelings for Paul grew. And she admitted after leaving the house that she only said it in the first place because she was feeling lost and vulnerable.

Helen, of course, survived that first eviction vote, but it was a further two weeks before love blossomed with 25-year-old Paul. The astute Bubble was first to pick up on the vibes. As they cracked open the cider for their evening meal, he told Helen, 'You never know, you and Paul might get it on later.'

Helen, still pining for Big G, was having none of it and made her 'sick' comment. She was also put off by the fact that Paul had been smooching with Penny during those awkward early days. Paul explained later that this was all one-way traffic and he'd had no choice but to go along with it because Penny had been so 'full-on'. He'd made it clear from the outset that he was single and looking for romance in the house.

And let's not forget — this is a man who has never been shy around women. Somewhat ludicrously, the £80,000-a-year car component designer even boasted of 'living the life of an international pop star.'

Right from the start, he was always keen to get the girls in the house involved in sex games. One of his early suggestions was naked Twister. The thought of bearing all in the chilly evening air didn't do much for the girls who were already wrapped up in woolly jumpers. Still, Paul was up for a saucy night and suggested he spin the wheel and 'get naked anyway'. Again, there were no takers.

Then, one night, Helen had dreamed about Paul. 'In the dream, Paul locked me in the bedroom,' she said. 'He told me, "You can't come out until you like me." Well, I'll never come out then!' Helen concluded.

His dream woman is tennis heroine Anna Kournikova. Blonde, bubbly and fun, Helen was as close as he was going to get to his fantasy figure in the house. Finally, asked which girl he'd like to sleep with most, Paul made his intentions clear by declaring without hesitation, 'H'. And he was quite encouraged by the fact that Helen made no secret of the fact that she was missing sex so much.

She'd talked with unabashed candour about the passion she shared with Big G before going on TV, making it clear that he more than lived up to his nickname in the bedroom. The dizzy beauty had even been

counting the days since they'd last
made love and wondered if the rest of
the group were hankering for it as
much as she was.

Bachelor Paul admitted it had
been two months since he'd last had a
romp and he appeared to be as
desperate for nookie as Helen. Soon,
he was stepping up his flirt offensive
and, by their fourth week in the house,
Helen finally started to melt.

Helen conceded later that her
early impressions of Paul were all
wrong. He wasn't a 'lad' at all — in
fact, he was kind and sensitive and
really not bad-looking. She was
particularly touched when he gave her
his Crunchie bar. And she warmed to
him even more over the dignified way
he coped each week as he faced
eviction — particularly when he was
up against Bubble in Week 5 and
everyone thought he was doomed.

'That's how I'll behave if they ever try to kick me out,' Helen thought.

As their flirting became more blatant, the other housemates began to pick up that something was going on.

Dance teacher Helen playfully rejected Paul's advances, but it was obvious to everyone that she was lapping up the attention, and her changing attitude was summed up the day Paul caught a sneaky peek of her boobs.

He accidentally walked in on topless Helen as she was changing in the bedroom. She shooed him away, but not before he got an eyeful in the mirror.

By the beginning of Week 5, Big G was becoming a fading memory for Helen and everything was set for the first proper *Big Brother* romance.

Paul showed just what he wanted to do to Helen by smearing 'I Love

Sex' across her back in yellow paint. And a siesta in the afternoon sun quickly developed into another heated flirt as the two lovebirds got frisky again.

Watching the action on TV, Big G, a 30-year-old salesman from Cardiff, finally cracked. 'I feel humiliated — I'm sick to death of it all,' he seethed to the *Mirror*. 'A man can only take so much. I really missed Helen when she went in and planned to propose when she came out.'

He ended their year-long relationship and said he'd no longer appear on any of the *Big Brother* TV shows.

Of course, neither Helen nor Paul knew this and, in their final three weeks together, the romance was full-on.

They frolicked in the garden over a choc ice, smearing each other with the sticky chocolate and vanilla ice cream. *Big Brother* bosses also played their part by arranging a romantic dinner for the six remaining contestants. Elizabeth and Dean talked longingly about their partners in the garden while Josh and Brian bitched happily in the living room. But the nation's gaze was firmly on Helen and Paul, happily ensconced in the cooler garden den, which Paul had begun calling his 'James Bond love shack.'

The dinner stunt brought howls of protest from family campaigners, who were horrified at the lengths Channel 4 executives appeared to be prepared to go to ensure two of the contestants had sex. Helen finally offered herself to Paul as they glugged down the final dregs of the wine. 'I love you! It's up to you, Paul. I'll let you do whatever you want,' she told him.

Sensationally, Paul lost his bottle

at the last minute. 'You're not really my perfect girl,' he said.

Helen pleaded with him to change his mind. But the moment was lost. Paul yawned and said he was tired.

Over the following days, however, they were back on track and developed their own language to talk about their relationship and the possibility of having sex. 'Stuff' was their word for love. They admitted their both saw 'stuff' in each other's eyes.

'Elvis' was the secret code name for sex. Why Elvis? Because when you make love, you wiggle your hips just like the King.

The young lovebirds retreated time and again to their den and Helen confessed to her pal Brian that she was longing for a 'bit of fun' — again meaning sex.

Then Brian asked the crucial question, the one every *Big Brother* viewer was asking: 'Could you really have sex?'

Helen replied, 'Without a doubt.'

They admitted they'd fantasised about having sex together. Paul claimed the talk of her boyfriend had held him back. He confessed that constantly being on TV had put him off, too. Then, in the most dramatic moment of the series, the two lovebirds disappeared underneath the blankets. Tantalisingly, they could be heard grappling beneath the orange covers. Were they at last about to do 'Elvis'? Would Paul, who'd boasted on his application form that he was hung like a donkey and humped like a rabbit, be man enough to see it through? No, he wouldn't. Helen admitted later that they hadn't even kissed under the blanket, though she did concede that he may have put his hand on her bottom.

Once again, Paul used Big G as an excuse, while Helen seemed more than happy to forget about him.

After his eviction, Josh Rafter said bluntly that Paul was using Helen because he reckoned their romance was a 'vote-winner.'

Anyway, the great saga came to a premature end when Helen and Paul were both nominated for eviction in the penultimate week. Paul had survived four evictions before, but he was no match for his TV lover. She easily won the vote and Paul was sent packing. In the harsh glare of the outside world, he was distinctly cool about the whole romance. Asked by Davina McCall if he had a special message for clearly besotted Helen, all he could say was, 'Let's meet for a drink when you get out.'

Paul told pals that he didn't think their relationship would last '24 hours' away from the house. He was relieved, too, that Big G hadn't been there to meet him at the studios.

Paul had worried about this continuously in the house, fearing they may have a fist fight over Helen. He also admitted later that there were two other girls that he'd had 'an interest in' before *Big Brother* and wouldn't say whether he'd choose Helen in favour of them now he was out. Things looked bleak for The Great Romance.

One of those girls, a very attractive brunette, was part of Paul's entourage at the TV studios. She told stunned production staff, 'I'm Paul Clarke's girlfriend, not Helen.'

But the girl, English and in her mid-20s, was in tears as Paul talked about his TV romance with Helen. And horrified by the sullen way he had come over immediately following his eviction, Paul softened his line.

In several interviews over the following few days, he declared undying love for Helen. Yes, he missed her madly. And yes, they had a brilliant future together.

So what had really changed his stance? Cynics have suggested that Paul realised that if he was going to ride the media gravy train for a few more months he'd have to stick with Helen. Togetherness was a better story, and to dump her now would confirm Josh's opinion that he was a two-faced schemer who had simply used the effervescent hairdresser.

The other view is that Paul was simply confused and bewildered on coming out of the house and had difficulty articulating his true feelings. Certainly, at his press conference after his eviction, he appeared 'double weird', to borrow one of his catchphrases. He found it impossible to talk coherently or even finish sentences.

Meanwhile, back in the TV house, Helen was hopelessly lovesick. She spent her first night away sleeping in his bed. She sniffed his pillow and talked fondly of how she could smell his hair wax.

Helen talked about Paul as though he were the hero of a Mills and Boon novel. Eventually, this was too much for her more wary housemates.

Elizabeth then felt the time had come to be honest with her. Reflecting on a conversation she'd had with Paul before his eviction, she told Helen, 'He said there was 60 per cent coming from you and 40 per cent from him.'

Helen was shocked by the news. 'Really?' she asked. She began to realise that her housemates might be trying to warn her about the future.

'He said he was unsure,' Elizabeth

replied. 'What an arse!' said Helen angrily. She said that she had no intention of putting all her eggs in one basket.

Paul, who'd had time to adjust with his family in Reading, Berkshire, greeted Helen when she left the house as runner-up to *Big Brother* winner Brian Dowling.

'All I can say is, "Oh my God!"' she said excitedly, impressed by Paul's well-scrubbed new image. Then she was presented with her dream Gucci handbag and matching shoes — a present from Paul.

'Oh my God! Paul Clarke! Words fail me!' she shrieked, but later she wouldn't be drawn on whether the relationship would take off.

'*Big Brother* will get back to you on that,' she said.

She was a little more forthcoming the next day after signing a six-figure deal with the *News of the World*. 'Thank goodness Paul left when he did because I do feel that passion would have got the better of us,' Helen said. 'We nearly did it when we were fighting over that choc ice. He smeared the chocolate coating on me and I looked up at him and thought, "Wow!" He gave me a flirty look, too, then we both put it out of our minds.'

Of their grappling underneath the blankets in the den, she said, 'I was tingling all over with excitement. Paul was turned on, too, and came out in goosebumps. The hairs on the back of his neck stood up. Nothing actually happened, but it was such a special moment for both of us. I was wrapped in the arms of a man who I thought was a right bit of all right. It seemed so funny because, in the first few weeks at the house, I'd thought Paul was a bit of a lad and he did nothing for me.

Then, a few weeks later, there we were, locked together. I really didn't want to have sex on TV, but you don't know what will happen when your senses are heightened. To be honest, what I really wanted to do in the house was to kiss him really passionately on the lips.'

There followed a fraught week as the two confused lovers tried to come to terms with their true feelings in the outside world. They were infuriated by press reports speculating on their relationship. And Helen reacted angrily when Paul turned up at the wrap party on the Tuesday after her eviction with an overnight bag. He'd done this because he was appearing on TV the next day and needed to change, but she wrongly assumed that he expected to bed her after the party.

'Don't treat me like a tart,' she

said angrily in a heated telephone conversation.

The pair were desperate to spend some quiet time together alone, away from the spotlight, but this was made impossible by the demands of their media deals. *Hello!* magazine were keen to reunite the couple on paradise island.

Helen and Paul rejected the free holiday — they didn't want their romance to be part of a 'media circus', they declared, though that was just what *Big Brother* had always been.

A week on — and many misunderstandings later — Helen was more hopeful that they did have a future together. 'I do feel the same about Paul as I did in the house,' she said. 'He's my boyfriend and I'm his girlfriend.'

Still they hadn't had sex, and they were angered by inaccurate reports of a mid-week romp at a London hotel. 'It's absolutely not true. We have not made love,' said Helen vehemently. 'It's stories like this that make everything so much more difficult for us.'

Days later, Paul was pictured kissing blonde model Louise Brill backstage at a fashion show that the pair had been judging in Reading. Yet minutes earlier, he had told a crowd, 'Helen and I love each other to bits and we're just going to take it slowly and see what happens.'

Helen said, 'We talked and he asked me how I felt. I said I was OK about it, but how would he feel if he saw me kissing men with their tops off? Paul tells me he wants us to go on national TV and tell the world of our love, but I'm not sure.

'One minute he's so loving on the phone and telling everybody, the next minute he's out on the town, or posing with models. I know what other people are saying about Paul — friends, other housemates, advisers — that he might not be sincere. But nothing anyone can say can change my mind about him.

'I can see everyone's point of view, but it doesn't change how I feel about him. I take people's points on board but I can't just say, "OK, I don't like him any more," can I? I can't change the way I feel. We're talking all the time, but it's hard.'

Helen was full of hope that they'd find happiness together in the future … and despite the ups and downs that are still to come, who's to say they won't?

CHAPTER 2

NAKED AMBITION – PENNY ELLIS

'It was never going to happen ...
He's just not man enough for me. He's a starter,
not a main course. But he was fun and
it was fun to flirt.'
PENNY ELLIS ON
HOUSEMATE PAUL

Trembling on the verge of a shattering orgasm, Penny Ellis dug her nails into the biceps of the giant who engulfed her and felt his muscles tighten as he exploded with her. The sensations ran in waves from her naked thighs to the tips of her breasts, and it seemed even her nipples were quivering with pleasure.

She may have been the first housemate voted off *Big Brother*, but if the consolation prize was nights of unfettered lust with Paul Mutagejja, a former Mr Great Britain, dubbed 'The Botty Beautiful', that was fine by her.

'We had the most fantastic sex,' she sighed, still feeling every delicious shudder. 'It was absolutely sensational. We made love all night and dropped off to sleep before waking up and having sex again.'

It was a world away from the rainy morning where Born-again Christian Penny, 33, dialled the Channel 4 hotline and waited patiently to be put through. The only problem was that she'd mixed up the *Big Breakfast* with *Big Brother*.

Teacher Penny wanted to get her class on television reading poetry they'd written. It would have been their big moment, a treat to remember.

'I was trying to call the *Big Breakfast* to see if I could get my schoolgirls on the show,' she explained. 'But by accident I got the

Big Brother hotline instead, so I left my name. It took me ages to send in my application form, but I thought I'd learn something about myself — and I have.'

As luck would have it, the *Big Brother* house was just a few hundred yards from the East London school where she was a popular member of staff.

Of course, there were warnings from her head teacher about behaviour in front of the cameras, plus the problem of finding a supply teacher at a cost of £8,000 to do her job while she was on unpaid leave.

But Penny — who'd long before changed her name from Lisa because she didn't like the sound of it — wanted to make a mark for herself. She'd gone to drama school, hoping for a career as an actress before making a living teaching at the Sarah

Bonnell School. She'd been there a decade, but it took just five days for her to make a national name for herself on *Big Brother* and have TV producers licking their lips.

It started when she got out out of the bath. The warm water was still trickling over her naked flesh, running in rivulets between her boobs. Penny was proud of her bust — she'd had it surgically enhanced from a 36AA to a C-cup — and, for the moment anyway, they held up the fluffy bath towel around her.

Perhaps it was a draught of cold air stiffening her nipples that shifted the towel just slightly, or perhaps it wasn't tight enough. Whatever, it fell to her feet and left her standing there, naked and glowing in all her 6ft glory on national TV. As she paused a little too long to pick it up, telly bosses knew they were on to a ratings winner.

Television executives could have edited out the footage before it was seen by viewers of E4 because of the 15-minute delay. They chose not to.

The apology they put out later, and the E4 logo covering her pubic hair, did the trick of plastering *Big Brother* all over the papers. Of course, a spokesman for the station said, 'We believe it was an accident when Penny dropped the towel twice.' But it was clear they were delighted.

For her part, Penny later told the *Daily Star*, 'I was a bit afraid about that, especially when I came out of the house and some of my Christian friends weren't there. I can imagine they're a bit cross about it. I'll be upset if I lost really good friends over it, but I was willing to be totally me. If, because of it, I'm known as a dizzy weirdo, then so be it. Thankfully, I had my breasts done. Otherwise, I'd have been mortified. I'd never do anything like that on purpose. I hope my pupils weren't watching.'

But there was no doubting her flirting and fumbling with housemate Paul before he turned his attentions to Helen. And when Penny jokingly suggested that she'd have sex on camera to win the £70,000 prize money, she finally found herself in very deep water with headmistress Cauthar Tooley.

Cauthar warned Penny that she'd be booted out of the girls-only school, whose motto is 'Learning for Life'. The head teacher always knew she might lose Penny to acting when she took on *Big Brother*, but she wasn't standing for any nonsense.

'If she wants to behave in a lewd way, she knows she'll have her contract terminated,' she warned while Penny was still inside the house.

Of course, straight-talking Cauthar knew she couldn't get her message to Penny, even though some of her class crept up to the *Big Brother* studios and shouted encouragement over the wall. To be honest, though, encouragement wasn't something Penny needed.

For five turbulent days her romance with Paul was *the* talking point around the country. But after an 'affair' consisting of long, lingering kisses, fondles and rolls in the garden, Penny dumped the younger man, saying that he was not in her league.

So what sort of bloke did she go for? Penny stunned her housemates when she revealed that she once consecutively dated four men over the age of 60.

There were mixed feelings in the group, but Bubble cut to the chase when he asked her if she could sleep with an old man.

Penny told him she found the older men very attractive because of their life experiences but refuted any suggestion of sexual intercourse.

It was this type of outrageous, drunken chat that had producers and bookmakers tipping Penny to last the full 64 days. But there was also behaviour that got the backs up of the other housemates.

House-proud Penny tried to dominate the kitchen. And when Stuart baked bread, it sparked off a huge four-letter row. Then there was the time she spent cleaning the cupboards in a leopard-skin bikini and rubber gloves.

Soon the group were conjuring extreme scenarios where she might reveal her dark side. Their imaginations ran wild. Dean came up with the idea that after a few weeks she'd turn into a horror film freak.

Certainly, as her behaviour became increasingly bizarre, Penny compared her eviction from the house to the kind of attention that Princess Diana had! More than a million viewers voted her out but, before she went, lovelorn Penny turned her attentions again to Paul. On her last day, she made several hapless attempts to snog him again. It happened when several of the housemates were preening themselves in the girls' bedroom in preparation for *Big Brother*'s live eviction show. Paul was trying on one of Brian's tops when Penny launched herself at him, falling with him on to a bed and rolling around.

Paul told her to go and pack her stuff before complaining of sexual harassment. He eventually managed to disentangle himself and crossed the room to check his ruffled hair in the mirror.

But it wasn't long before Penny was on top of him once more, smothering him with big wet kisses.

After separating, she flung herself at him a third time, dragging him into a dance around the room.

'Oh my God,' Paul mumbled.

It was probably a sentiment echoed in her school staff room.

Although she said she would be back teaching after the summer holidays, that statement always looked a little bit like Penny — mixed up.

Just days earlier, she'd declared, 'It would be a dream come true if the Royal Shakespeare Company called up and said, "We'd like you for our next production." '

She had also told her housemates, that it would be best for the school if she didn't go back.

Finally came the words Penny had dreaded, 'Penny, you have been evicted. Please leave the *Big Brother* house.'

After hugging everyone in turn, Penny admitted, 'You've made me aware of the things I've got to change. It's been a learning curve. I'm ready to go now. Thanks for putting up with me. I know I've been a bit neurotic.' Then she giggled, 'Well, a lot!'

She scuttled barefoot over the drawbridge and into the arms of presenter Davina McCall. Unlike some of the churchgoers scared off by her behaviour, Penny's pal Peter was there, reassuring her she was 'a household name'.

Then, as she was escorted into the studio, a sleeve of her dress slipped down and she giggled, 'All my clothes are coming off again!'

So what did Penny think of her housemates? 'When you got to their core, they were warm, but they were also tough and forceful with their words,' she revealed. 'But I love them all, I really do.'

When Davina asked about Penny's true feelings for Paul, she was immediately forthcoming. 'It was never going to happen,' she shrugged. 'He's just not man enough for me. He's a starter, not a main course. But he was fun and it was fun to flirt.'

On a final note, Penny revealed whom she thought would win. 'My bets are on Dean,' she said firmly. 'He seems to have it sussed. He's a lovely, lovely man — or Brian. He's fantastic!' She also predicted that Paul and Helen would become an item.

True to at least one of her comments, she did quit her teaching job — and it was then she fell for Mr Great Britain. Hunky male model Paul Mutagejja met Penny at a photo-shoot.

'His body is out of this world,'

she told the *Sunday People*. 'I couldn't keep my hands off him. When he took his top off, I just thought, Oh my God. He's gorgeous! We hit it off straight away. When the shoot ended, he asked me for my phone number and I was so excited. He called me next day and we met for breakfast — but ended up staying together for the whole day.

'We were walking through Leicester Square in the afternoon and he just stopped and started kissing me. It was very passionate and full-on. We stood there and kissed and kissed while all the tourists just walked around us. I felt like I was 16 all over again. My heart was thumping.

'I'd lost faith in ever finding happiness with a man. Taking part in *Big Brother* helped me sort my life out. It helped me come to terms with the past and move on. And it's made me ready for love again.

'I don't sleep with just anyone,' she said. 'They have to be really important. And Paul has made me feel sexy for the first time in years. Every time he touches me, I tremble. It's incredible. It's so nice to feel like a woman again — and wanted.'

Openly talking about her romps with Paul in a luxurious hotel, she added, 'It was amazing. It felt so right. At first when we got to the hotel we were both exhausted so I made us both a hot chocolate. Then we sat in bed watching a film. We could see the London Eye twinkling out of the window, then Paul just turned to me and kissed me. And we both got carried away.'

Penny has no hang-ups when it comes to making love. Just as marketing manager Fergus Ross discovered when she helped him unwind after a tough day at the office.

As he came through the door, she would be standing there stark naked except for a pair of tap-dancing shoes. Then, as he watched goggle-eyed, she would begin to dance, her glorious boobs jiggling in time to the metal taps on her heels. From there, his eyes would slip down to her sleek thighs, sliding against one another and parting tantalisingly briefly with each little kick.

'There were times when I'd be a little tired and grumpy in the evening, but if Penny was in a playful mood I wouldn't be grumpy for long,' Fergus told the *Sunday Mirror*. 'The sight of somebody tap dancing wearing only a pair of shoes is enough to make anyone look up from their work. It certainly makes it very hard to concentrate. I suppose you could say she knows how to get her own way.'

Fergus, who went out with Penny

for two years, added, 'She is an excellent tap-dancer. I think she was largely self-taught and she absolutely loves to perform. It's very natural for her.

'Getting sexually involved with Penny is like pulling the tail of a tiger. Any man who does so must be prepared for the consequences. She understands what men are all about and knows how to press the right buttons. Let's just say she's as talented behind closed doors as she is in the open.'

Fergus, 32, first met Penny through an old schoolfriend of hers. They finally clicked at a reunion party. 'I had no real idea she even fancied me,' he said. 'I thought she was after a friend of mine called Hayden but, as the evening progressed, it became clear it was me she wanted. At some point in the evening, I was walking up the stairs and she was walking down. As we passed she caught my eye and then just grabbed me and we started kissing. I couldn't quite believe it.'

They eventually made love at another party. 'There was a shortage of space at the party, if you get what I mean,' he said. 'I remember Penny dragging me outside to the front of the house where all the cars were parked. We ended up finding heaven in the back seat of a Ford Fiesta. It was all a bit of a laugh really. Penny basically knows what she wants and isn't afraid to ask. She's quite a forward person. She's one of those high-energy people. Put it like this — if there were more women like her, there'd be a lot less war.'

Fergus said Penny became even wilder after her £4,000 boob op. 'She'd always been unhappy with her breasts,' he added, 'and she always used to say things like, "When are they going to arrive?"

'She thought about it for a long time before having the operation three years ago and she did it for no one but herself. It was an image thing. She felt unhappy with the way she looked. Before the operation she was given removable implants to put in a bra to see how her new breasts would look. She was delighted with them and they were, to put it mildly, a huge boost to her confidence. She'd been slightly shy about her body before this, but after the operation she was a changed woman.'

Her new-found confidence soon became apparent when she went to a works party with Fergus a few weeks later. 'Penny turned up wearing a very revealing dress,' he said. 'It was definitely not the sort of thing she'd have worn before. She suddenly became the life and the soul of the party, dancing with everyone and very full of herself. From that point on, she really wouldn't wait for anyone else to start the party.'

As well as being worried about her breasts, Penny was also very insecure about her weight and was often on a diet. 'She spent several weeks on this detox diet and her skin ended up going yellow,' smiled Fergus. 'It didn't bother Penelope. She just laughed it off.'

The couple's two-year romance petered out three years ago but they still keep in touch. Days before she went into the house, they met to discuss tactics. 'Her aim was to be first off the block with everything on the show,' he said. 'She told me she'd basically do anything to win, even if that meant taking her clothes off or even having sex in front of the

JULES STENSON & LEWIS PANTHER

cameras. There are rules on the show as to what you can and can't do, but once someone broke the rules and it was open season on shocking behaviour, then Penny would have been in her element.

'She told me she might try and get off with one of the other married contestants to expose them as a love cheat, coming on strong to someone and then playing the innocent when they tried. Penny actually asked me if her having sex on the show would ruin our friendship. I told her it wouldn't and it was entirely up to her.'

Yet although Penny comes across as something of a sexual predator and an exhibitionist, Fergus said she is a much more complicated character. Penny became an active Christian while still at school and is now a member of an evangelist church in

London's East End. She has been involved in charity work for years.

'Some people might not be able to understand how she's a Christian on one hand and how she can appear naked on TV at the same time,' he said. 'But she sees nothing wrong with that. She has her own creed, if you like. She feels she's doing the right thing in terms of the talents she's been given. She knows she might lose friends or upset people at work but this didn't seem to bother her.'

One explanation for Penny's slightly odd character is her less-than-conventional upbringing.

Her parents, ex-RAF officer Brian Ellis and his German-born wife Aud, moved to Spain while Penny was at sixth-form college, so she lived alone in a small flat in Tunbridge Wells.

A friend said, 'She couldn't handle them and they couldn't handle her.

She never mentioned her father or mother at school, although they are now reconciled.'

Penny also has a sensitive and vulnerable side. 'On one occasion, before we began dating, she called me over a break-up with a previous boyfriend,' Fergus added. 'I went to meet her and she was, to put it mildly, distraught. I remember her whole frame was shaking. It was as if her world had fallen part — I've never seen her so upset. She thought this old boyfriend was very cruel to her. He had an affair and then announced he was leaving her for this new girl and that they were going to marry. It took her quite a few years to rebuild her confidence.'

Surprisingly, it was Penny's obsession with religion which caused her to break up with Fergus. 'There was three of us in that relationship —

me, her and God,' he said simply. 'She was very committed to her religion and, in the end, there was little time left for us. But if I have to come second to anyone, I suppose coming second to God isn't so bad.'

CHAPTER 3

LAMBORGHINI, LUST & LOATHING – STUART HOSKING

'It's unfair to say that I'm the new Nasty Nick ...
I was just winking at people in a friendly way ...
Sometimes it's a bit of a joke.'
STUART HOSKING

So what makes a Lamborghini-driving businessman go on *Big Brother*? When you've got three lovely children, an adoring wife and you're just about to move house, it's no wonder people think you're a little mad.

Stuart also chose to miss his son's second birthday and his seventh wedding anniversary and insisted he was in the *Big Brother* house simply so he could sit back and top up his tan. But like many of the things he and the rest of the housemates said, it wasn't exactly the truth.

The 36-year-old from the Oxfordshire countryside quit his job as a telecoms executive for a 'bit of a challenge', arrived in a suit and said he didn't need the £70,000 prize money.

Just as well, really. By the time he walked off the *Big Brother* set, most people saw him as one of the biggest posers in Britain. He lasted three weeks and was evicted with a massive 86 per cent of the vote, making him one of the most disliked people ever to appear on the show.

And by the time that happened, he was well and truly exposed as a man who would do anything for a bit of attention.

'I'm a poser and always have been,' said the 36-year-old. 'I still think I'm 25 mentally. I'm too directive and competitive and I guess that's what got me voted out, but I really am a nice guy.'

Some of his housemates would find that a bit hard to swallow, especially after their vicious rows during hot, drunken nights together.

The first full scale bust-up was with Penny. 'He's got a massive rod stuck up his arsehole!' she seethed, then branded him a 'fucking arse' after he told the group he'd sleep with all the girls except her. It was days before they called a truce.

But then Stuart did start again. When Penny was evicted, he turned his vitriol on lap dancer Amma.

Their war of words broke out on the eve of his eviction during a night of boozing to celebrate Brian's twenty-third birthday. With the gang all in boisterous spirits, tensions between the two rose as quickly as the bubbles in the hot tub.

Venomously, Stuart announced that he had a question for Amma, 'if you can answer it with your shallow mind.'

Amma sarcastically asked what the question was. But, as with many a drunken debate, the question never actually appeared!

The confrontation soon took another form as Stuart accused Amma of stealing his drink before sensationally claiming that he knew the vivacious housemate had voted for him to be evicted from the house.

In response, Amma then targeted Stuart's personality, telling him that he was a smug, insecure person.

The father of three then lowered himself into the hot tub to talk face-to-face, to tell her that he'd continue the conversation if only Amma wasn't so childish.

Amma hit back by saying that he

was the kind of man who gets upset when someone else has a better tan.

By now there was only one way to go. Amma stormed out of the water and into a bedroom.

Comforted by Josh, Narinder and Elizabeth, Amma wept her heart out and laid into Stuart once again. She told them how the conversation was really stupid. He made her so angry saying that he didn't agree with how she lived her life. She hoped the whole country would vote him out on Friday!

Although Stuart did later make an effort to talk to his irate housemate at 6.00am, both were too tired to reach a compromise. The soon-to-be evicted businessman did admit he was highly strung.

Everyone attempted to build bridges that lunchtime when an emergency session was called in the garden. Stuart was first up.

He told the house what a competitive person he was and apologised to Amma. He said that he didn't intend to pre-judge her in any way, and that she was a great person whose smile lit up the house.

Amma accepted his apology, though she remained in a bad mood. She admitted that she had said a lot of things she didn't mean, but said that Stuart was talking to her like she was 11.

Nor was she about to let him totally off the hook.

Bizarrely, Stuart went on to claim the only person he argues with in the same way was his sister-in-law. 'And I adore her,' he added.

After a brief hug, the rows seemed forgotten.

However, sun-mad Stuart had another, quite remarkable target for his sniping when he found out how Josh had a better tan than him.

After discovering that Josh used £12-a-time vitamin E and beta-carotene tanning pills, Stuart spat, 'He's not brown. He's just got carrot juice.'

An insight into the real Stuart come from his old drinking buddy Brynley Mason.

Brynley, 37, grew up with Stuart in Bicester, just a few miles north of Oxford. 'That smoothie on the telly is nothing like the Stuart I used to know,' he told the *News of the World*. 'Sure, he was always a poser. Everyone around here remembers him for the pink shirts and aftershave he used to wear. He has always come across as slightly superior.

'When we were all teenagers driving around in knackered old Escorts, he was there with a convertible Lancia. The last time I saw him, he pulled up outside a pub in his new Lamborghini. He had his shirt off and, as usual, was posing away like mad.'

Brynley went on, 'It must have been part of his show-off nature, but he was always pulling moonies. He loved having his picture taken in the shower, in front of the mirror and with his trousers down. All you had to do was give him a couple of drinks and off came his trousers.'

Luckily for viewers, Stuart kept his trousers on during the household's headline-hitting drink-fest when they downed six bottles of wine, six bottles of champagne and 20 litres of cider to say 'Bottoms up' to birthday boy Brian.

But he couldn't wait to drop his pants when he got back with wife Sian on his first night of freedom. Beaming like a cat who got the cream, he said the following day. 'I was so happy to see her. Going three weeks without sex was difficult. But we made up for it last night — in style with champagne.'

As the doors had closed on his adventure at Three Mills studios, where *Big Brother* is filmed, Stuart claimed he'd had a wonderful, fulfilling time.

'*Big Brother* gave me a great opportunity,' he said. 'But I was relieved to come out. I wanted to go back to my family.'

Then he turned to his search for a job. 'I'm open to offers,' he said. Denying he was a millionaire, the electrician's son went on, 'Stepping back from my career, I took a risk — it's probably a bit extreme, but it's one I don't regret.'

While he was inside the *Big Brother* house, he also let his wife oversee their move into a nine-acre

Oxfordshire farm.

'I wasn't born with a silver spoon in my mouth,' he insisted. 'I left school with a couple of O-levels and I've worked bloody hard for everything I've got. Nothing has been given to me. I come from a working-class background, though my mother will kill me for saying that.'

He also went down as one of Britain's biggest winkers, though he denied he'd tried to turn contestants against each other with his sly eye contact.

'It's unfair to say that I'm the new Nasty Nick,' he said, referring to the infamous villain of the first *Big Brother* series. 'I was just winking at people in a friendly way, I've always done it. Sometimes it's a bit of a joke. It's just a mannerism I've got. I obviously need to change the public perception of me.'

Mind you, Stuart let wife Sian do the talking when it came to defending his tattered reputation. The dark-haired 34-year-old laid the blame for his eviction on the girls in the house.

But she admitted she barely recognised the man she saw on TV as her husband and said a cocktail of booze and sexual tension inside the house had puffed up his arrogant image.

'Stuart's a lovely man,' she told the *Sunday Mirror*. 'All my friends adore him. It's rubbish to say that he has a problem with women. When he takes the kids to school, he chats to all the mums in the playground.'

And in a swipe at Amma and Penny, Sian added, 'Stuart was being kind and nice to them. I think the women had a problem with him, not the other way around.'

She did concede, however, that 'I

was surprised at him. He kept trying to make it up to Amma. I think that's because we have a rule in our marriage that we don't go to bed on an argument. But when he insisted on trying to sort out the situation, I just thought, "Oh my God, you've had too much to drink — go to bed. She's not going to accept your apology, so sort it out in the morning."

'He obviously had a lot on his mind. It was our son Rory's second birthday, he was missing us and there was the pressure of being in a house with nine other people. Stuart wasn't the man I know and love, but I think that Amma misinterpreted him. He was trying to say they all came from different backgrounds and I think she thought he had everything handed to him on a silver plate, which isn't the case.

'I also think, from the two

arguments he had with Penny and Amma, that they'd confided in him and regretted it afterwards. Stuart's very good at talking to people and getting to know them. They probably opened up in a way they wouldn't always do and he brought out a side in them they had hidden or didn't know about. They felt backed into a corner and attacked.'

Smooth-talking Stuart promised to treat everyone to a garden party after they left *Big Brother*, but it remains to be seen if the gang will all turn up.

He labelled Brian and Narinder 'immature' and said, 'Helen is a lovely girl but she's very young for her age and we haven't much in common.'

But desperate not to look too much of a baddie, he added, 'There was no one in the house I really disliked, and Dean, Paul, Bubble and Josh are all the sort of people I'd have a beer with. Paul is a bit of a lad but he reminds me of how I was when I was his age.'

Which gives another big clue to the reason why Stuart went on *Big Brother*, and why he didn't last long.

At 36, and with a happy family, he was never going to risk the saucy flirting that Channel 4 was hoping for during this series. But that didn't stop Elizabeth coming on to him, said Sian.

She told her husband, 'Elizabeth flirted with you outrageously,' and sighed, 'I thought the pair of them would get on because they are very similar — competitive and more mature, really.'

When he saw himself on TV for the first time, Stuart cringed as he watched footage of a few choice moments with 27-year-old Elizabeth.

He said he hadn't spotted any come-ons. 'I'm stupid Stuart,' he confessed, 'I never saw any of that.'

Elizabeth, who listed her three favourite things as 'sparkly stars, joss sticks and Vaseline', was shown licking her lips and arching her back as she asked Stuart if he'd considered his prospects for a *Big Brother* romance.

Another sequence showed Stuart bandaging Elizabeth in a first aid challenge and asking, 'Does that feel better?'

She purred, 'It does now.' The pair were also shown chasing each other with hoses in the garden.

When he'd walked away from the show, Stuart let out a cry of joy, shouting, 'Yes! Excellent! I'm going home!'

Unfortunately, his joy turned quickly to dismay as he walked staight into a row with neighbours when he arrived back at his new spread in the village of Murcott, Oxfordshire. He had left instructions for workmen to shield the home with a 6ft fence, but as one local put it, 'Perhaps he thinks he's going to become such a celebrity that he'll need to be protected from hordes of screaming fans. But the bungalow is half-a-mile from the nearest house so there's absolutely no need.

'It did have glorious views over buttercup meadows, fields and copses. Now the only view will be the back of a bloody great fence. You'd have thought after being cooped up on *Big Brother* he'd be yearning for the open spaces. Maybe he's got used to being penned in.'

Out of his last job and into a new home, Stuart hasn't had much time to get used to anything. Like many *Big Brother* contestants before him, he fancied a job as a television presenter.

So far, the only thing to emerge is his own website.

CHAPTER 4

SINNER & SAINT — NARINDER KAUR

'I can't wait to bonk my husband's brains out.
I was hard in the house — and I was a real bitch.'
NARINDER KAUR

It was the most explosive moment in Narinder's life. After years and years of searching in vain for fame, she finally felt like she had one hand on the prize.

And it was, ironically, also a moment of failure. For Nasty Naz, as she became known to millions, had just been kicked out of the *Big Brother* house after 29 days.

Recalling the moment when Channel 4 minders had to pull her away from the screaming crowd,

Narinder said, 'It was better than sex, better than getting married, better than anything I've ever experienced. I doubt I'll ever feel anything like it ever again.'

Naz had arrived. The self-proclaimed bitch was going places. She said, 'I want to see my name up there. The billing will be Martin Luther King, Indira Gandhi, then Narinder Kaur.'

If she ever does achieve lasting fame, it will be on the back of being one of the most foul-mouthed and obnoxious *Big Brother* contestants there has ever been. From the start she declared, 'People taking a pop at me will not affect my confidence at all. Absolutely not. Bring it on. I've been through so much in my life that it doesn't bother me.'

When she faced the gangplank of the public vote, she simply

announced, 'It's not been a barrel of laughs in here. I'm not bothered.'

Naz finally managed to calm down after a night of champagne-fuelled sex after her eviction. After four weeks suppressing her deepest urges she confessed, 'I can't wait to bonk my husband's brains out. I was hard in the house — and I was a real bitch.'

Naz's public announcement about her need for marathon lust clearly angered religious leaders in her native Leicester. The sultry 28-year-old had proclaimed on the hit show that she was a strict Punjabi Sikh. But holy men at her local temple watched horrified as she flashed her bare bottom on TV and snogged gay housemate Brian.

And they'd warned her that they were waiting for her with heavy penances, involving cleaning the shoes of every worshipper who leaves his footwear at the door.

One furious temple member said, 'She will have to prove how penitent she is in front of everyone, and if that means she has to collect and clean shoes, then so be it. She flouted her beliefs by drinking heavily, revealing private parts, and playing sex games with another man when she is married. If she was genuinely strict then she probably wouldn't have gone into the house in the first place.'

It's not surprising they were upset, and the constant referrals to her toilet habits would not have helped matters. Even in the first week, she was openly admitting that the lack of her favourite curry had left her blocked up. The problem even warranted the use of laxatives. And when Naz needed medical attention for tummy troubles, she openly boasted about how she flirted with the GP.

Naz would seemingly do anything, however undignified, for fame. And the Channel 4 show and its £70,000 first prize was her last desperate grasp at it after 700 rejections since the age of 12.

She had been passed over by Channel 4's youth programme *Network 7*, *Coronation Street*, the *Big Breakfast*, GMTV, MTV and the Asian comedy series *Goodness Gracious Me*. She admitted, 'Some of the time you send in scripts or a video and don't hear anything. I got an audition to be a presenter on the *Big Breakfast* but I never heard from them again.'

Still, she did have one brush with movie stardom after she took part in *Cafi 21*, a programme for young Asians. She was also spotted by Bollywood director Sunny Deol and whisked off to Bombay to play a part in the romantic drama *Dillyagi*.

She said, 'It was a small part but it gave me a taste of what I hope is to come. But I want to make my name in Hollywood. Why should I have to go to India to be famous? I should be recognised here. There needs to be a role model for young British Asian women.'

After the *Big Brother* explosion, the £30,000-a-year medical rep now wants wanted to be an MTV presenter, or link up with housemate Brian to become the next Richard and Judy.

And she was backed by her husband who said, 'Life after *Big Brother* may be a good opportunity for her. I think she'd be great on TV and I know that's something she'd love to do.'

In fact, that's exactly why Naz went on the show in the first place. She admits, '*Big Brother* was my final chance. I said to my husband, "If nothing comes of this, I'll give up and start a family." '

But Naz's irrepressible ego and supreme self-confidence did not come naturally to her. They are the results of the 'overt racism' she battled against during her childhood in Tyneside where she was the only dark-skinned pupil at her school.

After her A-Levels, Narinder went to the University of Derby to study law. 'I had no intention of being a lawyer — I saw it as a way to get my independence and get away from Tyneside,' she admitted.

Like other contestants, she had to send in a video explaining why she wanted to be in *Big Brother*. In typical Narinder style, she told the producers, 'Forget Nasty Nick, forget Sexy Mel — I'm going to spice up that house.'

Husband Jatinder said, 'If it takes off now, I'll give up my career and become her manager.' And although he's desperate for children, he adds, 'Narinder has to have a go at this now or she'd always resent me for it.'

Narinder's not so keen on starting a family, but she concedes, 'Even film stars manage to fit these things in between movies. I'm sure we'll find a way.'

Although her quest for fame hasn't taken off so far — apart from on *Big Brother* — it wouldn't be a surprise if she eventually cracked it, judging by her determination. Because when she really sees something she wants, Naz makes sure she gets it.

The scheming Sikh even stole her husband from under the nose of another woman. She said, 'He was engaged to a girl from Coventry but that didn't stop me.'

As soon as she saw Jatinder Punia ten years ago, Naz knew she was going to marry him. The girl who has blasted all her former housemates for being boring, stupid or two-faced told the *Mirror*, 'I had never had a boyfriend before. This guy was nice, sexy and good looking. I knew this was going to be long-term.'

'We kept seeing each other and snogging, then he'd remember that he had a fiancée and it would cool off for a bit.' But Jat kept coming back for more and after six months decided to finish with his fiancée and go for Naz.

However, their seven-year marriage nearly came a cropper over her husband's laddish behaviour. The couple were actually living apart when Naz applied to go on *Big Brother*. They only got back together after Jat, 30, vowed to put an end to his partying. Naz admitted, 'We were arguing so much that we decided the best thing to do was to separate. It was just before Christmas and it all came to a head over an argument about Jatinder's drinking when he came home at 6.00am one day after a night out at his mate's. I ended up throwing my wedding ring down the toilet. Luckily, I didn't flush the chain.

'Jatinder went to live with friends. There was never a moment when I stopped loving him and I always thought we would pull through it, but I felt devastated and there were a lot of tears.'

The couple say they are now determined to make their marriage work and are living together again at their detached £160,000 home in Oadby, outside Leicester. It is to be hoped that the air inside is never as blue as it was when Naz was in the *Big Brother* house. When she was evicted, she really went to town on her housemates.

First to face her wrath was the then

2-1 favourite Bubble. Narinder moaned, 'His point of view is crap. He is Bernard Manning. I had my biggest problem with him. Bubble is a real sexist pig. He thinks he's great and spends all his time saying how funny he is. But the sad thing is, he hasn't got a funny bone in his body. Some days I just felt like grabbing him round the neck and shouting, "Get away from me."

'And I hated the way he used to make a joke of my religion. After I told everyone I was a Sikh he joked, "We seek her here, we seek her there." He didn't know when to stop and had a vicious temper which I'm sure, outside of the house, will have landed him in a fair few fights. I don't believe he's really a racist. He made just the one comment and I gave him one of my glares and put him in his place. He was certainly a young, white and confused male who did not understand a lot of things about me. And he also had this terrible habit of stealing the pieces of paper on which the *Big Brother* tasks were written — obviously so he could try and sell them afterwards. Whenever he went bare-chested I was repulsed. Josh has magnificent pecs, but Bubble's nipples go down to his belly.'

And when asked about Helen, at first Naz said, 'Urghhh. She's immature, she's seven years old and she can be bitchy. She's Joan Collins. She struggled with my name and only got it right because everyone started calling me Naz-three letters, which is about her limit.

'She's still finding herself in the big wide world. She's 25 going on 7 and I didn't like the way she would go behind my back whingeing about me rather than telling me it to my face.'

Now her view on Helen has

changed. 'I'm coming round to the opinion that, despite all her faults, deep down she's a great girl,' she said.

Next she moved on to Paul, saying, 'He's really pretty but there's not much up there. He's an all-rounder but boring. He was like a cushion for everyone — if you cried he was there for you, but there was no personality there. I asked him to tell me about his life and he just drooled in a monotone. He was also lazy. He saw me chopping onions one day and I had tears streaming down my cheeks, but all he could think to do was open a tin of spaghetti.'

Amma, according to Naz, was 'deceptive. She's got a game plan more than anyone. She makes out she's great with everyone, but she's not. She gets on my nerves. The day before nomination she was all over you, the day after she didn't care about you. She also had this horrible habit of putting everyone's leftover food into tin foil and popping it into the fridge to nibble later. She'd scavenge anything. It repulsed me, she acted like a filthy pig.

'And she was damn lazy. She couldn't understand why she should be forced to go without cigarettes when we we ran out because she said it was an addiction. She got in a foul temper and it was unfair on the others. I wanted to hit her when I saw her sitting wrapped in that orange blanket she carried with her everywhere — that's all she does. Sits in an orange blanket and picks at food.'

Narinder said of Josh, 'I'm suspicious of his motives. I stuck up for him and he nominated me. We called him Mr Motivator. He was lovely to look at, but I feel he was disappointing. He was brought in to spice up the house as this fun disco person and all he did was bury himself in his book, look up and sigh when there was something he didn't like going on and play backgammon. He probably didn't get on with most of the group and I suppose that's not surprising.'

And Dean, according to Naz, was 'boring. He bugged the hell out of me. He said nothing at all that stimulated me. He spoke to Helen like she was two years old and he liked that.

'My abiding memory of him will be that crappy guitar of his. There was no room for it and that tai chi he used to practise with Elizabeth was something else. They were reading out of books, for goodness' sake. And he might have been spending all his time doing weights in the garden, but I've got more biceps than him.

'I know he loves his girlfriend to

JULES STENSON & LEWIS PANTHER

bits, but it was as if he was scared of women. He had this terrible medicine which he said he needed to control his rampant sex drive, but he just struck me as a lump of lard. He was the most boring person in the house and very condescending. I know Helen was immature and acted like a seven-year-old, but he used to treat her as if she was two.'

Narinder's vitriol was spared on Brian, though. 'He was great. He was my sanity. Paul and the others used to say, "What's your husband going to think?" about what I was getting up to with Brian, but I knew he wouldn't mind. Without him, I don't think I would have survived.

'People have criticised him for being immature and spoilt, but I don't think he is. He went too far in the argument with Josh, but I understand him. He felt under threat because, as the only gay in the house, he felt he wasn't being judged and that all collapsed when Josh came in. He told me gays like Josh don't get on with gays like him and I'm sure there'll be no romance between them. But I think he's great for the house and he will go far. I know he wants to win.

'We were constantly thinking of ways to get the ratings up, like pillow fights. We've already got our futures mapped out. We're going to do MTV and *Richard and Judy* together.

'And people are spot-on when they say he's the new Graham Norton. He's very, very funny. But people should also remember he is sensitive and vulnerable.'

Of Elizabeth, Narinder observed, 'She was nice, but she would get a bit bitchy, especially in the kitchen when she wasn't being left to do things as she wanted. Some of us were there to have a laugh, but she was there to win. She was never nasty to me, but I got the feeling she was a dark horse. While she was very willing to discuss other people's lives and other people's problems, she always backed off revealing too much about herself.'

Geordie Narinder was uncomfortable with cameramen filming her every move. She said, 'I was a bit reluctant to strip the first couple of days and I felt awkward having a shower knowing the world was watching me. But Amma was very confident about her body from day one. She'd be sitting on the bed in the morning legs akimbo shaving her bikini line without a care in the world. It was cut for TV but I'm sure the cameramen got a right eyeful.'

Narinder admits she didn't think she was going to be voted out. 'I thought I would make it to the last four because several people in the house had virtually no personalities. I got bored, but it was because they were so boring. I didn't need sleeping tablets — I just had to speak to them.'

But she admitted, 'I don't think I would have won. I don't think Britain is ready for a woman to win, let alone an Asian woman — but I so think I was the fall-guy.

'There were two groups that formed. I was getting very close to Brian, but people would never have voted him out because he was gay and they knew there would have been a massive backlash from viewers.'

Even though she failed to win the £70,000 top prize, Naz said she had no regrets about her *Big Brother* experience. As for the reaction of the Sikh elders, she insists she was not being a hypocrite by praying one minute then simulating sex with gay

Brian the next. She said, 'I'm upset that the Sikh community are upset with me, but surprised. I don't think I've done anything wrong.'

But she admitted, '99 per cent of Asian families would have been horrified at what I've done.'

For the moment, Narinder hopes the aftermath of *Big Brother* will bring her the fame she craves, as it has done for previous housemates. Her ultimate ambition is to become a film star as famous as Gwyneth Paltrow or Sharon Stone. 'I'd really love that,' she says.

CHAPTER 5

SEX, DRUGS AND MADNESS – BUBBLE

'It's been very hard and there have been times
when I've broken down and cried
with my head in my hands. The moment I walked
out of the house, the world around me changed.
Sometimes I wonder what the hell I did
by going into the house.'

BUBBLE

He was the first contestant to walk into the house — and many thought he would be the last out.

Bubble — real name Paul Ferguson — appeared to have all the qualities required to romp away with the £70,000 first prize. A laugh-a-minute, down-to-earth Cockney joker with a heart of gold. What more would the viewers want?

Certainly, there were similarities in Bubble's story and last year's winner,

Craig Phillips. Craig, 29, had gone on the show to win money to pay for an operation for his Down's Syndrome pal Jo Harris, 19.

Bubble, 25, made it clear that he wanted to win to provide a 'better life' for his three-year-old daughter Briony — to make sure she wanted for nothing.

He tugged viewers' heartstrings by being filmed playing with the blonde toddler in the park in the very first Channel 4 show on *Big Brother II*. The message was clear — vote for me and the lovely little girl gets all the dosh.

But while Scouser Craig, after surviving several early nominations, became more popular as the show went on, the opposite happened with Bubble. He was moody and, at times, irritating, particularly when his jokes backfired. Still, no one thought the nightclub boss would be evicted from the house after just five weeks.

The bookies had Paul Clarke as a 10-1 on favourite to get the boot. But, for once, the bookies got it a horribly wrong and, in the biggest surprise of *Big Brother II*, Bubble was out.

All the housemates were stunned. Brian, in particular, was distraught. He looked at his TV pals and asked, 'Do the viewers see the same things as me?' The lovable Irishman was also worried. If the viewers had rejected a loud clown like Bubble, what chance did he have, he thought?

Hat-loving Bubble consoled himself with the fact that the viewers liked him more than Paul, but in the end he'd lost the beauty contest to the hunky car designer. After all, many of the voters who determined the fate of the contestants were teenage girls.

Still, the fun and games were only just starting for Bubble after his eviction. Unknown to him, his long-term love Stephanie Johnston, 23, had been cheating on him while he was locked away with an old flame, 25-year-old painter and decorator Steve Summers.

The affair had been going on for two months, having started before Bubble went into the *Big Brother* house. Steve said they'd enjoyed 'fantastic sex' together and they were even pictured kissing at a secret rendezvous.

How was Stephanie going to explain all this to her sex-starved boyfriend who'd pined for her all the time they were apart?

The dramatic confrontation happened just minutes after Bubble took the long walk down the *Big Brother* gangplank. Stephanie was in the studio audience as presenter Davina McCall gave the chirpy

Chelsea fan the grim news, and newspaper articles revealing the affair were revealed on screen.

Terrified that he'd dump her there and then — and miss out on her 15 minutes of fame — emotional Stephanie told a clearly confused Bubble, 'You know it's a pile of pants. You know I love you. I wouldn't do that.' It made for fantastic TV — one of the most dramatic moments of the series.

But was Steph telling the truth? Bubble, clearly in need of some tender loving care, decided to give her the benfit of the doubt. After all, they'd met when they were both working punishing late hours at Surrey nightclubs and they'd come through a lot together.

'I love my girlfriend,' he said simply. 'I love her to bits.'

Away from the cameras, though, there was a heated exchange between the warring couple. Stephanie briefly fled the studios in tears and was seen wandering around a car park looking bewildered. She was also smoking furiously.

But Bubble did forgive her, and buoyed by a £45,000 newspaper cheque for his life story, the pair finally enjoyed a passionate reunion at a London hotel on the night of his eviction.

'We had a great night and I shagged for Britain,' smiled Bubble. 'Wouldn't you if you'd been in that house for five weeks?'

Sadly, this particular love story did not have a happy ending. Just four days later, while Bubble was enjoying his new found-fame at the *Tomb Raider* premiére, Steph was with a muscle-bound club doorman.

She met burly security boss Mark Evans, 29, for sex at a London hotel just moments after waving goodbye to gullible Bubble. Ex-RAF fireman Mark was described by pals as a 'legend with the ladies'.

Bubble dumped Steph immediately. 'I gave her three years of my life but the trust has gone from our relationship,' he sobbed. 'A lot of things have obviously gone on and it has all happened as my world has been turned upside down by *Big Brother*. This is the time when I really need her most and I can't believe it has happened. I'm all on my own now. I haven't done anything wrong and can't believe she's treated me like this.'

He wasn't broken-hearted for long, though. Just a few weeks later, he was spotted smooching with a new blonde at a London club.

Bubble has found his new-found celebrity more difficult to handle than the other contestants. All received counselling from the show's resident psychologist Brett Carr after they were evicted. And the final four housemates also had secret counselling from Brett while they were inside the *Big Brother* house. These were the only scenes throughout the entire series which weren't filmed.

But long after leaving the TV house, Bubble has continued to seek help from Brett. 'Sometimes I just wish for my old life back,' Bubble said sadly. 'It's been very hard and there have been times when I've broken down and cried with my head in my hands. The moment I walked out of the house, the world around me changed. It feels like *The Wizard of Oz*. I've been to sleep and woken up in a different land like Dorothy. Everyone knows who I am and wants a bit of me. Everything I do is hassle.

Simply walking down the street to buy cigarettes is a struggle. I'll get at least ten people coming up to me. In nightclubs it's hard, too. Sometimes I wonder what the hell I did by going into the house. I'm not just Paul Ferguson from Surrey any more, I'm Bubble.'

The one person who has helped keep his feet on the ground is daughter Briony, from his relationship with former fiancée Gemma Lenderyou, 23.

'I was prepared to put my life under the microscope and be dragged through the mud so that I could improve my daughter's life,' he said. 'I'd given up valuable time with her and knew my past with drugs and drink-driving would be exposed. But I was happy to do it for her. It never entered my mind that I wouldn't be walking out the winner.

'When I was told I was out, it was

as if someone had put their hands down my throat and ripped out my insides. I realised then I'd made a terrible mistake going into the house. I'd lost six weekends with Briony for nothing. What an idiot.'

Bubble also revealed that he'd come close to killing himself over drugs and his boozing — but was saved by the love of little Briony.

'I started drugs at about 16 — smoking draw (cannabis) with mates — and then did LSD. I started to go clubbing and moved on to Ecstasy and then cocaine and speed. I overdosed on vodka and LSD when I was 16 and was taken away in an ambulance. I was always pushing myself to the boundaries.

'I spiralled out of control after I split with Gemma and lost the perfect family I'd started with her and Briony. I spent thousands of pounds on drugs.

I'd sit alone in my room, take the full-length mirror off the wall and spread cocaine all over it. Then I'd chop it into dozens of lines and spend all day snorting it and then not be able to sleep. I started to lose weight and looked terrible.

'I'd confiscate drugs from people at the nightclub where I worked and then sneak off and do them myself. It was madness.

'It finally came to a head on Millennium Eve when I broke down. I cried and told my parents I had a problem and I was killing myself. I was at my lowest point. I'd lost my credit cards, my car, my flat and my family. I said to myself that without Briony I wouldn't be here — I would have ended it.'

Now his 'must-have' drug is nicotine. When he ran out of cigarettes in the house, he pleaded with *Big Brother* for nicotine patches or gum, saying, 'If I give up, I could become a bit tetchy.'

He was driven to despair when he also ran out of cigarette papers and, in desperation, made a metal smoking pipe from a sweetcorn tin. To his disappointment, *Big Brother* confiscated it.

Bubble is the youngest of four sons to dad Jimmy, 59, and mum Anna, 55. A hip disorder meant he spent life as a toddler in plaster. But despite a suspension for truancy, he left school with six GSCEs.

At 17, after working at McDonald's, he spent a year in Australia with his brother, James, 36. 'I slept with loads of girls,' said Bubble. 'All you say is, "I'm English," and they strip. I suppose in all I've slept with about 100 women — it's the gift of the gab. I haven't got the looks but I've got the talk.'

He even once boasted of bedding a hooker on a wild weekend with pals in Amsterdam. But he confessed that he was so out of it he can't be completely sure whether they had full sex.

Bubble's colourful past made him one of the first stars of *Big Brother II* to capture the viewers' imagination. The lively lad from Surbiton, Surrey, left his parents at the doors of the compound with the fond farewell: "See ya, Mum! See ya, Dad!' Then, dropping his coat on the sofa, he looked around the house before shouting his first words, 'This is so cool!'

Within minutes, Bubble partially revealed the origin of his nickname. 'Well,' he told the other contestants, 'it could be because of my bubbly personality or it could be to do with bubble bath or it could be because I once farted bubbles into a pint glass through a straw.'

Bubble was never happier than when he was playing a practical joke on his unsuspecting housemates, especially Brian. His repertoire included removing slats from beds, breaking wind in pillowcases, rubbing toothpaste in sheets, pretending he'd been hypnotised, hiding housemates' belongings and throwing pillows, balls, rice and anything else he could get his hands on at Brian in bed.

Bubble also confessed to quitting a job once because they wouldn't let him wear his beloved hat behind the bar.

He also admitted that he has a hat for every occasion and had brought ten of his favourites into the *Big Brother* house. Each one apparently had a name.

It wasn't immediately clear

whether he'd leave his hat on for sex, but love-making was clearly on his mind when he admitted to Amma that he'd eagerly have sex on TV.

Amma simply laughed at his enthusiasm and assured him that she didn't need sex 'that badly'. But, by now, Bubble was on a roll. He maintained that he might go for months without sex so he might as well get it whenever he had the chance.

It would all make his later outrage at his cheating girlfriend seem a bit rich.

Still, Bubble revealed a deeper side to his character when he told the group of his penchant for writing poetry. The other great love of Bubble's life is soccer. He announced that it was like a religion to him. He was desperate to find out the score when, in preparation for England's vital World Cup qualifier against

Greece (2-0 to England, for the record) he even went for a radical change in appearance to show his support for his country. Dean took on the role of barber as he hacked away at Bubble's hair with a pair of clippers. Bubble had asked for the St George's Cross, but ended up with more of a Beckham-style mohican.

Two weeks into the show, Bubble celebrated his twenty-fifth birthday. Now a birthday never went uncelebrated in the *Big Brother* house and Bubble's special day was no exception. As the group prepared their evening meal of pilchards, the birthday boy emerged from the Diary Room to announce they were going to have a 'Football Blues Party'. Bubble could not contain his excitement. 'I gotta paint me face! Fuck the pilchards!' he cried. The party passed off uneventfully, partly because there was no alcohol.

Bubble also attempted to play matchmaker between Brian and the other gay contestant, 32-year-old Josh. Josh was voted into the house after two weeks when Penny became the first person to be evicted.

Bubble was convinced that the Irish Romeo had a secret hankering for the new house hunk.

Even Bubble, however, had to take things easy when he hurt his leg in an accident during a Boogie Nights dancing task. But he was soon given the all-clear by the *Big Brother* doctor and almost won a place in the Guinness Book of Records for chewing corn!

The group gathered around the dining table as Bubble attempted to scoff down the 169 kernels in just three minutes. Three attempts brought him close, but not quite close enough, as his nerves got the better of him. Still he is officially a UK record holder having chomped 165 kernels in the time-limit.

Bubble became the fourth contestant to leave the house when he lost the eviction vote to Paul Clarke, polling 534,574 votes to Paul's 470,058 in the closest contest of the series.

Shocked by the news, Bubble broke down in tears. But as the group offered their commiserations to the master prankster, Bubble put on a brave face and said in a gentlemanly manner, 'It's been a pleasure.'

His face ashen with shock, he wasted no time in going to pack his case. Fellow nominee Paul was equally surprised, anticipating his own eviction.

In a high state of emotion, Bubble broke down again only seconds later in front of Elizabeth. 'I was here for the money,' he mumbled through tears, talking again about his plan to provide for Briony. 'I just wanted her to have whatever she wanted,' he cried.

He then went round each of the remaining housemates to give them his honest, but fair, appraisal.

Paul: 'I don't think we got on as well, but I like you.'

Helen: 'You're fantastic with a great zest for life, and I never had a bad thought about you.'

Josh: 'You're mad. Anyone who spends £2,500 on a pair of trousers has no idea of money, and you borrowed my hat without asking. But you taught me how to play backgammon.'

Elizabeth: 'You're a diamond and I love you to bits.'

Amma: 'You're a star, very laid back, and a one-on-one is better with you.'

Brian: 'You are, without a doubt, the funniest man I've ever met, and you made it a lot easier for me being in here.'

Dean: 'He comes from the Black Country and he's a treasure!'

Later, he blamed his eviction on his looks. 'Paul's a good-looking bloke,' he said philosophically. 'And I've never done well in the facial department!'

CHAPTER 6

WATER PISTOLS, STRIPPING & SNOGGING – AMMA ANTWI-AGYEI

'I was always being offered money for sex
but I never accepted it, …
My price would be a minimum of £1 million,'
AMMA ANTWI-AGYEI

Naked Amma ran her fingertips slowly between her glistening breasts and provocatively downwards as rivulets of water cascaded over her velvet skin. Out there, in the darkness of the strip club, eyes leered at her stunning, shapely form as she cavorted for them. She drove them so wild that soon she would be offered £25,000 for sex by a wealthy businessman.

But she would turn him down. For deep inside, Amma was still the daughter brought up single-handedly by a strict Seventh-Day Adventist mum. Her mother thought she was working as a librarian, but Amma had opened up a new and secret chapter in her life, earning up to £400 a night in the table-dancing clubs and strip booths of London. She performed naked under waterfalls as kinky men, who had paid £30 a time to watch her, shot at her pert nipples with water pistols.

After experiences like that, being under the gaze of the nation in the *Big Brother* house was, so to speak, water off a duck's back.

Amma entranced millions by snogging Elizabeth and had us howling with laughter on the sofa as she belched and broke wind as if she didn't have a care in the world.

She may have seemed easy meat. But as a middle-aged businessman discovered in the darkness of a Mayfair club, brainbox Amma — with nine GCSEs and three A-levels — is no pushover.

'I'll give you £25,000 to sleep with me,' he growled.

But it would have cost him much, much more to bed the beauty brought up on state benefits.

'I was always being offered money for sex but I never accepted it,' 23-year-old Amma told the *Sunday Mirror*. 'For me to accept, it would have to have been a life-changing offer because I would find it so hard to live with myself afterwards. My price would be a minimum of £1 million, but I'm anything but promiscuous. I've only had two or three serious boyfriends and I've slept with far fewer people than anyone else I know.'

The irony that she's a lap-dancer but has only had a few fellas just about sums Amma up perfectly. Her upbringing tells the same story. Despite living in the poverty trap, she clawed her way to a fantastic education. Yet Amma Antwi-Agyei turned to stripping.

It certainly helped fund a lavish lifestyle which she dreamed of during her childhood. Home is now a £1,000-a-month, trendy, one-bedroom flat in a complex which has its own restaurant, gym and shop in East London. It's a stark contrast to the cramped flats her mum rented. Neighbours include city high-fliers, television producers and models. There's even a TV star living there now.

Amma insists her step into the murky world of stripping was a spur-of-the-moment decision. She took it after stumbling across a newspaper advertisement for 'dancers.' But during

Top left: The romance that kept a nation on tenterhooks – what does the future hold for star-crossed lovers Helen and Paul?

Top right: She loves Gucci, but she loved the housemates more: big-hearted Helen chose a party over Gucci gifts on her birthday.

Bottom: The Big E for Big G: Helen kisses him goodbye…and soon moves on to a new romance!

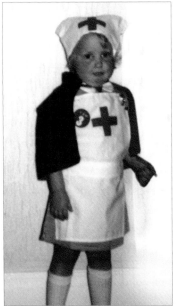

Helen's sweet charm was obvious from an early age and, below right, she demonstrates an early penchant for hairdresssing.

Top: The Big Brother bedroom, a melting pot for sleep-talking, pillow-fighting, whispered secrets and late-night shenanigans.

Bottom: Girl action. Things got steamy when Elizabeth, Amma and Helen got naked and oily in the jacuzzi.

Top: A remarkable pair. Brian and Narinder had an unmistakable chemistry…but Naz's bitching got her the boot, while lovable, quick-witted Brian emerged victorious. Will they become the new Richard and Judy?

Bottom: Late-comer Josh caused Brian's emotions to boil over in a series of sizzling arguments.

Top left: Despite her bikini-clad kitchen cleaning and towel-dropping antics, Penny failed to win us over and was the first to be evicted.

Top right: The new Nasty Nick? Stuart's argumentative side caused trouble in the house...but Sian knows him better...

Bottom left: Bye bye, Betty. In the house she was the mother hen, but her boyfriend revealed a saucier side to the 'dark horse'.

Bottom right: Big Daddy Dean leaves the house, to be reunited with his beloved Vanessa.

Top left: Big Brother will get back to you…the famous Diary Room chair.

Top right: Bold, brassy Amma, never afraid to speak her mind…or to let her body do the talking!

Bottom: 'I love blinkin', I do.' Helen's quirky comments became catchphrases up and down the country.

Top: Bubble's moods swung high and low, but his love for daughter Briony (*centre left*) remained constant.

Bottom: Stories of Bubble's wild lifestyle were constantly making headlines.

Top left: If she could see you then…

Top right: Paul and Helen blissfully reunited and (*bottom*) constantly attracting media attention.

her time in the *Big Brother* house, it became clear there was more to it than that. She admitted she suffered from a lack of confidence and took to the stage as an ego boost. But then Amma also hinted that she had taken cocaine during one of the group chats, which were mainly fuelled by drink. And like some of the boasts of her fellow contestants, it has to be taken with a pinch of salt.

A few days after seeing that newspaper advert, Amma was at the Berkeley Playhouse in Mayfair for an audition. There she was judged by Britain's first-ever Page 3 girl Jilly Johnson and *The Bill* actress Samantha Robson, herself a former table dancer.

'Suddenly, the backing track from the James Bond film, *Goldfinger*, came booming out,' laughs Amma. 'I wanted to burst into laughter. Still, I got on stage and danced down to my bra and knickers. I was useless but they told me on the spot I was hired.'

Amma began to dance at the club four nights a week and took advantage of coaching sessions from the older girls. At that club, the girls just danced down to sexy underwear. Garters, suspenders and stockings — all the male fantasy trappings.

'At first, I didn't have a clue,' she told the *Sunday Mirror*. 'I was disco-dancing around the stage like a mad thing. The other girls taught me how to slow down and be sexier. I got good at it but I never felt turned on. It's a silly job. You drink, you dance, chat to people and go home.'

There was definitely no sex, though. Just like *Big Brother*, really. Amma gave viewers the impression there was more to her than meets the eye when she appeared to flirt with Elizabeth during her time in the house.

But she insists she is heterosexual and has a healthy respect for men, despite being leered at night after night.

In fact, Amma and Elizabeth's soap-covered erotic performance on Day 35 would have proved a sight for sore eyes to the audience she was used to before *Big Brother*.

Amma and Elizabeth had got intimate on the sofa – a kiss and a cuddle that seemed to have an immediate impact on them.

Amma asked Elizabeth if she would have a problem sharing the bath if she said she was bisexual. Elizabeth answered that it wouldn't be a problem even if she was a lesbian.

But afterwards, Amma tried to pour cold water on her sensual show. 'I'm as straight as they come. I like hot-blooded men as much as the next girl,' she claimed. 'I'm not into women, although I can appreciate a beautiful woman.'

And she certainly did when she later enjoyed a lingering snog with the snooty girl from the other side of the tracks during one of the steamier nights on *Big Brother*.

Before long, Amma (Ghanian for 'born on Saturday') was spilling the beans about her secret life, vigorously defending her choice to lap dance. By Day 6 of her stay in the house, she was treating the others to the tricks of her trade.

But it's all come to an end with *Big Brother*. 'For my mum's sake, I've given it up. I don't want to hurt her any more,' she said.

It's easy to see why she has so much respect for her Ghanian mother after she struggled to bring up Amma and her four siblings on her own. She was widowed when her husband, part-time taxi driver Mensah Antwi-

Agyei, was hit by a speeding car when Amma was just four.

To add to the heartache and hardship, her mother was pregnant with her younger brother Nana, now 18. She suffered a back injury which forced her to bring her family up on the dole. They moved from a council flat in Watford, Hertfordshire, to a semi in Golder's Green when she was five.

But times were still tough. And it was a particularly harsh upbringing for Amma who found herself being mercilessly bullied at secondary school.

'It was hard,' she sighed. 'Other pupils used to call me "tramp" and "fleabag" because it was clear my family had no money. My mum made sure we wanted for nothing but I sometimes had to wear my sister's hand-me-downs and there was no money for fashionable clothes. I didn't have a lot of friends and at that time I didn't stand up for myself and so I became an easy target.'

In her second year, following intervention from her furious mother, Amma moved to another school, with a new resolve to stand up for herself. And that certainly showed during her rows with Stuart, especially as she admitted she could have punched the aloof businessman when he picked on her during the infamous Jacuzzi screaming match.

But proud Amma is guarded against making too much of her poverty-stricken roots. 'I don't want to make my life out to be a hard-luck story. My childhood was happy because my mum did a good job of being both parents. We were poor but we never went hungry or anything. My mother even worked as a cleaner in my school to ensure we could go to after-school clubs and for music lessons. She never remarried. It was something that made me determined never to be caught in the poverty trap. There's no reason to be like that if you apply yourself. I also learned to live on limited funds.

'When I left school, I worked as a shop assistant and had various waitressing jobs. I wasn't thrilled with what I was doing. It was so boring.'

Then she spotted the lap dancer advert.

'There's a big part of me that's a closet performer, the hairbrush-singing in my bedroom and always wanting to be the lead in school plays. I like entertaining people, making them laugh and smile. And table-dancing was just something completely different from anything I'd done before.'

So, like many a professional,

independent woman who's seen it as a quick and easy way to pick up cash over the past few years, Amma turned to dancing. And even being sprayed by water didn't faze her.

She told the *Sunday Mirror*, 'It was just a bit of fun and an alternative way to table dance. More than anything, I felt silly and I often find myself laughing. I think some guys did get a kick out of spraying me. Maybe it was a power thing and it was certainly the closest they got to touching you. But I think most other men just thought it was silly and a laugh.'

She says the leap from dancing in her underwear to topless dancing was bigger than from going topless to completely naked. 'I am self-conscious about my breasts and so going topless was the hardest.'

On the whole, and in spite of her

penchant for breaking wind and burping, Amma was probably the most timid of all the contestants trying to pocket the £70,000 prize money.

However, during one of the few intimate chats she had, she told Helen about her boyfriend and how she was dying for sex with him.

On Day 41 of her six-week stay in the house, Amma finally opened up about her man. As she was facing eviction, the often quiet housemate chose to confide in the Welsh lass before drifting off to sleep. She revealed that the first thing she'd do when she got out would be to call her man, who she had been seeing for three weeks.

Helen then grilled the nominated contestant for in-depth details and discovered Amma's lover is very skinny with a ginger beard. However, Amma declined to respond to Helen's last question about the size of his manhood. And even after she was evicted and faced a quizzing from Davina McCall, she kept mum. 'It is a new relationship,' she conceded. 'He works in the graphic design world. He's neither rich nor poor. He's nice, and that's all I'm saying.'

But she did admit she was looking forward to having sex again. With a mischievous grin, she admitted, 'I missed it as any person would. There weren't a great many opportunities in the house to release any kind of frustration. From day one I withdrew into myself because there were so many strong characters in the house. I am argumentative but nowhere near as aggressive as I looked on TV.'

Although Amma managed to keep her eyebrow-raising occupation as a table-dancer a secret from her mum Juliana for two-and-a-half years, she realised it wouldn't last once she went on national television. And, like Brian, who revealed he was gay to his parents just before he went on the show, Amma decided to come clean just before *Big Brother*.

'Telling my mum what I did for a living was one of the most heartbreaking things I've ever had to do,' she confessed. 'I knew she'd feel I had let her down. I hated myself for the lies I'd told my mum but I wanted to protect her from worrying about me every single minute of every single day.'

So two days before she walked across the East London drawbridge she can see from the trendy flat she has bought with her earnings, Amma broke the news, 'I'm a stripper.'

Amma went on, 'She thought *Big Brother* was fantastic, but she broke down in floods of tears when I told her

I took my clothes off for a living. She was devastated. I was so sorry for disappointing her but I didn't want the truth coming out on national television.

'She couldn't understand why I did it and still doesn't fully. We didn't row. She cried and I talked. Thankfully, she phoned me the next day and told me she loved me no matter what I did. That was so important to me.'

But she has no regrets about her choice of career. 'I hate strippers who go on *Trisha* moaning about being exploited. I liked what I did and most of the men I danced for were nice, polite and friendly.'

When she became the the fifth person to leave the *Big Brother* house 43 days after she walked into the television spotlight, Amma was still a bit of a mystery. The sultry 5ft 7in beauty, who says *Tomb Raider* star Lara Croft is her heroine, was full of contradictions. Despite being the voice of reason during the late-night debates, it was her unreasonable belching and 'bottom burping' for which she was probably best known, especially after she had feasted on one of Narinder's curries.

And although she claimed to be a tough cookie, showing off her fiery temper on the night of Brian's twenty-third birthday, she wasn't that hard-nosed. After drinking a wee bit too much cider, Stuart snapped at Amma after she'd joined a debate between the boys.

Despite this confrontation — which she parodied so well — the sensitive side of Amma has often been suppressed.

A shocking four-letter argument with Stuart ensued, and it was clear she was in desperate need of a shoulder to cry on. It was Dean who got the job. He comforted the tearful Amma in the den as she pored over the evening's events.

Afterwards, Amma revealed that she'd have 'hit Stuart' during their drunken argument if it weren't for the 24-hour surveillance inside the *Big Brother* house.

Her frank confession came as testosterone levels raged inside the house during a group discussion about fighting. Amma speculated whether all the squabbles in the house would have become physical if the housemates hadn't known they were on TV.

It wasn't clear how serious Amma was with her threats of physical violence. Neither was it clear which big, life-changing events had occurred in Amma's life until after she left the house because she refused to talk about them with the other housemates.

But she had no such problems talking about her bad habits, even stopping a game of tennis in its tracks on one occasion with one of her explosive 'wind-breaks'.

In a candid conversation with Helen and Paul about the etiquette of 'picking and flicking', she admitted to eating the fruits of her nose!

The closest Amma came to confiding in the fellow contestants about her harsh upbringing came when she revealed she was plagued by bad luck. As time was running out for her towards the end of her six-week stay, she revealed that every time she got close to winning something, fate intervened to keep the prize just out of reach. Dancing medals, film tickets and singing awards have all been offered to Amma, but a tragic run of bad fortune has kept her from getting her hands on them.

Amma lightened the mood many times on *Big Brother*, though. On top of her table-tennis-stopping stinks, Amma managed to provide Elizabeth's funniest moment of her stay during a game of volleyball.

In the middle of a particularly demanding move, Amma's left nipple managed to negotiate its way out of her bikini top, leading Elizabeth to claim it to be the most amusing thing that had happened in the house.

Once Penny and Narinder were booted out, Amma, Elizabeth and Helen bonded. The trio went as far as getting naked to share a hot bath together during Elizabeth's pampering party.

Amma will also be remembered for being one of only three smokers in the house. A lack of tobacco can cause most smokers stress, and she was no different after losing her stash.

But her rolling expertise did come in handy when she showed Paul how to make the perfect rollie, building a bridge between the two housemates' disintegrating friendship in the process.

As for the nominations, Amma remained reasonably consistent in her voting. She selected Paul every week, although the irony is that he outstayed her, and tended to reserve her second choice for whichever contestant was causing her grief that week. But the most revealing thing about her came during her post-eviction interview. Clearly overcome by the occasion, Amma struggled to find answers to the opening questions as to how she was feeling. But after coming to terms with sitting in a studio rather than the house, Davina got down to the basics.

'What do you think is the people's perception of you?' asked Davina.

'No idea. Honestly.' came the response.

Amma was even more forthcoming with assessing her own image in the house. 'I can be quite aggressive,' she admitted. 'But temperamental? No!'

But that was nothing compared to her overall view of life in the *Big Brother* house. 'I felt I wasn't myself,' she began. 'I did feel overpowered by the other people in the house. I had to be more forceful and it tended to be the negative side.'

And what did she think about the others?

Josh: 'I like him but he's very serious. I nominated him because I felt there was tension between us.

Bubble: 'The only other person who was honest in there. He's a bit loud and edgy but has a big heart.'

Brian: 'He's a joker with a huge heart. He kept the tempo up and made sure we didn't take it too seriously.'

Elizabeth: 'The house mother, everyone's confidante, really caring. Not a bad word to say about anyone.'

Helen: 'My favourite. A sweet lovely, bubbly woman who gets on with everybody. A big heart, too.'

Dean: 'He's the father figure and group organiser. Intelligent, very sensible. We weren't very close.'

Stuart: 'We had one big disagreement and he was only in the house for two days after that.'

Narinder: 'She spoke without thinking and could have offended people — it's very easy to do in there!'

Paul: 'He's lovely but parts of him do grate and annoy me. Housemates think the public love him.'

Penny: 'We had a row after arriving

but then she wasn't there long.'

CHAPTER 7

MUSCLES, PASSION & FASHION – JOSH RAFTER

'I had never been to a gay club.
I was in the middle of the floor on my own
and this guy just kissed me ...
for some reason I said I'd give him a lift home.'
JOSH RAFTER

Gay Josh Rafter promised a wicked whirlwind of lust and laughs which would rock the Big Brother house. So thousands voted him in. But the only thing the ex-millionaire managed to drag off to bed was a good book. So the nation booted him out.

Josh's pledge of 'naked naughtiness' was guaranteed to flop from the start — and from his first step inside the house, he knew it. They had already got to know each other really well, and then I came in,' he revealed later. 'They had established little cliques and in-jokes. Unfortunately it was something I wasn't part of.'

The 32-year-old self-confessed fitness fanatic was determined to prove he could spice up the *Big Brother* house and claim the £70,000 prize money. But viewers quickly discovered that the only thing Josh really knew how to spice up was his vegetable curry. He was so sure of his ability to succeed and scoop the jackpot that he told pals, 'Bet on me.' And it should have been a doddle. After all, the man who boasted of 'making a million and losing a million' had already managed to reinvent himself beyond recognition.

A master of self-promotion, Josh sold himself as the party-animal viewers were clamouring for. He told *Big Brother* bosses, 'I always give satisfaction. I know I can give good television.'

Before being chosen from three people in the phone vote, Josh planned his *Big Brother* bid like a military campaign. While he hid out in Portugal with fellow hopefuls Natasha Simpson, 27, and Anne Edgar, 45, his faithful friends rallied the gay community for support. London's cafés and bars were plastered with posters of the muscle man, urging people to choose 'Josh and Pecs'. His mates even teased that he would seduce fellow gay housemate Brian.

So *Big Brother* should have been a piece of cake for the bronzed Adonis who strolled through the Diary Room door on Day 16 of the contest. But not everything went according to plan for the talented manipulator. After a few weeks cooped up with strangers, Josh retreated into his shell.

To be fair, the hunky property manager certainly did cause a stir as he was led blindfold into the house on his first day to face screams of shock from the unsuspecting group. The girls were immediately impressed with his chiselled good-looks and perfect 6ft physique. The boys were clearly stunned. Within five minutes of Josh's arrival in the house, Helen and Narinder had swept him off on a hand-in-hand guided tour.

Grinning like Cheshire cats, they were pleased as punch with their hunky new playmate before he uttered the magic words, 'Do you want a beer?'

Outside, newspapers were crammed with tales of Josh's wild, roller-coaster lifestyle. Pals revealed lust-crazed nights with countless lovers and steamy sex sessions in nightclubs. On one occasion, fun-loving Josh even dressed in drag as Posh Spice and conned a group of drunken lads into snogging him.

His boss revealed, 'The staff parties are wild and that's down to Josh organising games. Before you know it, you're sloshed and doing silly things.'

But inside the compound, it wasn't all fun and games for the handsome North London lad. Josh quickly discovered it would take more than a few luxuries to win over the *Big Brother* boys eyeing up their unexpected competition.

Bubble and Paul were both wary of the new housemate, choosing to light cigarettes and wander silently out to the garden moments after he had arrived. As the girls opened beers and toasted their new beau, Dean followed the lads outside.

Josh then shocked his new

housemates by announcing that he was gay. Helen and Narinder seemed more disappointed than surprised. After all, they had just wasted hours flirting with him.

The revelation came over lunch as the group grilled Josh about Anne and Natasha, the two rejected *Big Brother* contestants. Helen none too subtly asked if he had shagged them.

It was then Josh revealed he wasn't that way inclined!

Before the day was out, the girls decided to analyse Josh's role in the house. As they recalled the attention they had lavished on him, Helen said simply, 'I don't think the guys like it.' She had hit the nail squarely on the head.

Of course, Josh now had Brian to contend with. Throughout his time in the *BB* house, there was always a tension between the two gay men.

From the moment Josh strode into the kitchen, the girls were forced to reassure him that he was Number One.

Josh said later, 'I went in there with every intention of livening things up. I'd only been in there a few days and then there was that huge row with Brian who admitted he was having a problem with having another gay guy in the house. After that I just withdrew and went into myself. I decided to just quietly try to get along with everybody and not make a big fuss.

Josh's entrance into *Big Brother* brought plenty of surprises, and none bigger than the present he unwittingly gave the group.

After being called to the store room, he was instructed to read out a cryptic note to the house which told the housemates to look under the garden's rockery and discover a mystery gift. As the rocks were cast aside, the surprise was gradually revealed. Lying in wait for the past two weeks, slap-bang in the middle of the garden, *Big Brother* had hidden a hot tub.

But there was confusion from Brian, who seemed unable to grasp the general implications of hot, water, tub and garden.

Then Big Brother announced that the water still had to be purified, meaning there could be no hot-tub action before Sunday. But it would see plenty of use over the coming weeks, proving well worth the wait.

The Jacuzzi stunned the nation, but nothing could compare with the jaw-dropping shock of Josh's £2,500 Gucci trousers. The new boy stunned the group when Stuart asked, 'What's your most expensive item?'

Embarrassed, he admitted thst it

was the Gucci trousers. Paul and Bubble, in particular, were incredulous.

Later, the fabled trousers got an airing in the boys' bedroom, prompting an eerie silence. Nothing too remarkable about this, except that Bubble was in the room.

On Day 17, big spender Josh impressed the housemates with tales of his amazing lifestyle and extravagant spending habits. As the group were ushered into the girls' bedroom while work was being carried out on the hot tub, Amma, Narinder and Helen flicked through Josh's personal photos.

One of them was of his stylist — who used to cut the Spice Girls' hair.

Having travelled all around the world in his property job, Josh told the house he is a proud member of the Global Disco Family, a network which attends Gay Pride events across the world.

As Amma rifled through his toiletries bag, it became clear that only the best will do. Could he cope with going back to basics in the house? Josh casually mentioned that he once spent £12 on a tube of toothpaste. He also told the group he was 23 when he first kissed another man.

Narinder was clearly stunned and asked if he went from straight to gay in one night.

'It was a progression,' explained Josh.

He said he had made 94 phone calls and went on six blind dates before finally telling his family he was gay. He said his dad had told him that he had not turned out as he wanted him too.

Narinder asked Josh what he was hoping for from the show. He admitted that he didn't think the UK was ready for a gay winner. Stuart warned him that everyone would have an opinion of him. People would believe what they read.

But Josh said he was prepared for all eventualities. He didn't care what people wrote about him.

Clearly under the influence of an earlier cider binge, Helen asked who he would sleep with in the house, male and female.

Remembering how their last discussion on the topic had caused friction when Stuart listed four girls but excluded Penny, Amma warned him that he didn't have to answer. It would only cause arguments.

Looking uncomfortable, and referring to the men, Josh answered bashfully that none were his type. After a pestering from Helen, he admitted he would sleep with Amma.

Clearly drunk after six glasses of

cider, Brian felt slighted by this choice. He even went so far as to call Amma a whore.

But just three days after he entered the house, Josh's honeymoon was over. When the new housemate was safely tucked up in bed, Brian, Narinder and Helen joined together for some late-night gossip. He announced that Josh was really not his type.

Helen agreed and — surprise, surprise — stated the obvious, saying how posh he was.

Narinder was quick to jump to his defence, but Brian warned her that it was only day three. Her opinion might change.

Loved him or hate him, the man had clearly made an impression.

Josh convinced himself that Brian's outbursts, which came to a head in an astonishing row between the two men, could have been the result of his own behaviour. In a heart-to-heart with Amma, he tried to make sense of the Irishman's feelings towards him. 'I don't know why he hates me,' he said.

Amma explained that it bothered Brian that everyone got on really well with Josh, who was very young for his age. She added that the two of them could be mates!

Josh then predicted his future in the house. He expected to be nominated on Monday.

Next day, Josh revealed why he had taken so long to get out of bed and join the housemates' conga, causing them to fail the task. He admitted having had 'a huge stiffy'. 'It was ridiculous. I really need some sex.' He revealed that when he was in Portugal, he'd been 'five-knuckle shuffling twice a day'!

Josh and Brian were soon at it

again when they played Chase Me around the garden and pulled each other's pants down. Josh pulled up the Irishman's bathrobe, exposing his nakedness.

But Josh was the only housemate not to wear a bathrobe. Instead, he chose to parade around in a pair of tiny shorts and Brian seized the opportunity to grab at his boxers and pull them down.

Surprisingly, Josh didn't seem to mind. He took his time pulling his shorts back up and appeared to be enjoying their frolics, although the tensions continued to simmer beneath the surface. The two men's long-overdue showdown finally arrived on Day 42.

Earlier that evening, Brian had told Elizabeth and Dean that he was ready to approach Josh.

Incredibly, at the same time, Josh

was having a similar coversation with Amma.

That night, they finally got their opportunity to talk. Alone in the bedroom, Josh confronted Brian.

'It's like the world revolves around you,' he said. 'I'm a stranger coming into the house and within a few days you attack me verbally.

'I had no one to talk to. I thought these were all on your side.'

Brian hit back, 'It's not about sides. I've been here longer than you but that doesn't give me the right to feel I can walk all over you.

'I find it more insulting if you just sit there and don't find it funny.'

Josh was unimpressed by Brian's defence. 'I give you mocks back,' he said. 'But you just say I'm grumpy.'

Brian thought about this. 'I think you think that what I say can change people's opinions of you,' he said. 'It's not like that in here.'

But Josh carried on, 'It's to do with you being a bitch to me,' he told him. 'I have seen you get ratty with me. The other day you blew hot and cold.'

Brian hit back, 'I'm not going to let myself be matched with a guy who happens to be gay for the amusement of half of England!'

Brian then went on to claim that Josh took him too seriously, while Josh insisted that Brian couldn't take what he dished out.

As Dean and Paul interrupted the pair on their way to bed, they did manage to find something to agree about; they will *not* be keeping in touch after they leave the house.

On Day 47, Josh revealed he had dabbled in the occult, and even believed he was a clairvoyant. He said that he had got into the use of Ouija boards.

Even his friends were aware of his ability to reach the other side. One of them warned him, 'There is something about you and you are going to lose it.'

Josh also revealed he had sought advice from a clairvoyant when deciding whether to enter the *Big Brother* house. The psychic had recommended he should not take part in the game show, but he ignored her warning.

Josh went on to explain that a Tarot reading had warned him that someone in the group would betray him.

He even admitted he had consulted a white witch, whose predictions had been very accurate. Unable to hold his tongue any longer, Brian teased his sparring partner's faith in mystical powers.

But Josh wasn't finished. He then

claimed he had been involved in devil worship!

If his plan was to send a chill down their spines, it worked; almost every wall in the *Big Brother* house is covered with a huge mirror. He said that some people called mirrors 'the devil's looking glass'.

Brian screamed and Helen announced that she was definitely sleeping in the boys' room that night.

While Brian squirmed, Josh teased him, until Elizabeth piped up and asked if he was a worshipper?

Josh admitted he was 'involved', but refused to elaborate.

On Day 49, Josh confessed he had wanted to leave the house on his first day because he had found it a struggle to fit in. Outside, he had made promises of 'nudity, nocturnal activities and naughtiness', but adjusting to life in the house had proved much tougher than he had expected.

The housemates appreciated his honesty, reassuring him that they had tried their hardest to accommodate the newcomer, even though Dean thought he was a plant.

On Day 50, Josh finally swaggered down the Walk of Shame to the tune of Right Said Fred's smash 'I'm Too Sexy'. After much deliberation, he had chosen to wear his red-striped Gucci shirt and jeans. Overwhelmed by the crowd, he was led into the studio to talk about his experience in the house.

'It's incredible!' he told Davina as he watched the housemates live on the big screen. 'I can't believe it! They're eating my bread!'

Josh said he wasn't surprised by his eviction because he'd been pitted against Welsh beauty Helen, whose relationship with Paul was escalating fast.

'It was mad and bad,' he said. 'They were with each other all the time and there were innuendos. I'm told it was a big friendship and they are having a laugh. We thought there might be a few headlines.'

Talking of blossoming house romances, Josh was quizzed about his relationship with Brian. 'You rendered Brian speechless,' said Davina, referring to his oral sex proposition during their candlelit dinner-for-two. 'Did you fancy him?'

'Not at all,' said Josh. 'I was winding him up. It was pay-back. I was in control. It was good fun. But the argument made it difficult to talk. I don't understand the backlash; I think he felt threatened.'

Josh said he had found it a real struggle to form meaningful relationships with the others because they had already bonded. 'I was suppressed in the first week,' he said, citing his clash with Brian as a reason for not being able to deliver his bold early promises of naked lust live on screen. 'He was a nice guy, but he has a lot of growing up to do,' he said.

He admitted the housemates had never got to know the real Josh and was shocked when he discovered that Paul had branded him a 'slimy, poncey type'.

'It's his ignorance,' said Josh as the crowd cheered. 'He's really stupid.'

As the interview came to a close, Josh admitted that the only person he really liked in the house was Elizabeth. He said she had taken him under her wing, and listed Elizabeth and Dean as his favourites to win.

'I didn't expect a lot out of *Big Brother*,' he told Davina, summing up life under the cameras. 'But it was a great experience.'

CHAPTER 8

SLEEP-TALKER & INTERNATIONAL POP STAR – PAUL CLARKE

'If I took a girl out on a date for dinner,
I'd pay. But if after the third date she hadn't even
offered to go halves or pay for the meal,
she wouldn't be my type.'

PAUL CLARKE

Ladies' man Paul Clarke was picked for *Big Brother* because of his outrageous boasts about sex. He told stunned Channel 4 bosses, 'I'm hung like a donkey and shag like rabbit.' He bragged of bedding dozens of girls as he lived 'the life of an international pop star'. Not bad for someone who designed components for cars.

Big Brother producers were keen to up the sex content in the second series of the show and were terrified that viewers would switch off if a couple didn't have sex, as they have done in virtually all the European versions of the series.

It was thought that Paul, more than anyone else, could provide what they craved more than anything else — a *Big Brother* bonk.

Certainly if his past sexual conquests were anything to go by, he was unlikely to let them down. His friends breathlessly recalled outrageous tales of excess. Best pal Rob Ryan told how Paul had once bedded a German trainee nurse — and then compared notes about her sex performance with her boyfriend. Paul, 25, did the deed while working as an £80,000-a-year freelance car designer in Cologne.

Rob, who has known Paul since their days at Bournemouth University and worked with him at Ford, told the *Daily Star*, 'This girl was absolutely gorgeous. She walked into the bar where we'd go for a drink near where we lived. She had legs stretching on for ever and she really got us going in a rubber nurse's outfit with a red cross across her boobs.

'Paul said to me, "God, she looks really sexy. I wouldn't mind her feeling my pulse." She had this skin-tight dress with a spilt right up the middle. Everyone in the bar was looking at her but Paul had the guts to go up and start talking to her.

'People didn't see this side of him on *Big Brother* but he can be really charming when he wants to be and this girl just fell for him big style. The girls in Cologne are the best-looking in the world but the blokes are really dull, so when they meet someone like Paul who's got a little charm and wit they're up for anything.

'They're all really tall and fit. It

usually takes a few dates to get them in the sack but Paul nailed this girl that night. I can remember her walking out with Paul looking like she had won a million. He'd spun his magic and she didn't realise it. I saw him leave the room and look over his shoulder and give me the look which said, "I've scored!"

'The next day he came into the bar with a big smile over his face. He said she was absolutely insatiable in bed and she kept him going all night. "She was a wild," he said. "She's a nurse and she examined every inch of my body." '

Rob, from New Barnet, Hertfordshire, recalled that about a week later the same woman came into the bar, this time with a man. 'Paul wasn't bothered about her going with another bloke so he went up and started chatting to him,' Rob added. 'This bloke also turned out to be a Brit working in Cologne, too, so Paul asked how he knew her.

'When this guy said he'd been seeing her for a few weeks, Paul nearly choked on his beer. He said, "Sorry, mate, but I had her last week." This guy wasn't bothered and asked, "How was she?" Then they just had a real laugh and a giggle about how good she was in the sack.

'This girl was stood in the corner with her mates looking over. She must have realised what they were going on about because she didn't seem too happy.'

Rob travelled to London on every one of the five weeks his mate was nominated for eviction on *Big Brother*, and he has news for Helen Adams, who fell in love with the romeo on the TV show.

'Paul got off with about 30 or 40

girls while was in Cologne with me,' he said. 'He doesn't do relationships, he's too young to be tied down. The world's his oyster.'

Paul became a babe magnet after an operation on his big ears! They had blighted his teenage years and undermined his confidence. So to boost his self-esteem, Paul had them pinned back when he was 16.

'One of the most important things in my life was that operation,' he said to the *Daily Star*. 'Once I had them done, I suddenly had this overwhelming response from girls. It was incredible that something like that was happening to me.'

'Parents always say the sweetest things to their kids,' he said. 'Mine told me I was a good-looking lad and I shouldn't worry about things like this. But in my heart I wanted the op. I can still remember how painful it was. I was actually awake during it and could hear them doing the cutting. It was awful. I was in pain for about three weeks afterwards, but it was worth it.

'I was so proud of the result. When I saw myself in the mirror afterwards I was really excited. I met up with a group of friends and everyone was like, "Wow — oh my God." It was a huge boost to my confidence. I really couldn't have predicted the overwhelming response I got from attractive girls. That was all new to me.'

A few months after the op, the inevitable happend — Paul lost his virginity. He was 17. 'I met this lovely girl and we ended up going out for about six weeks,' he said. 'We knew it wasn't going to be serious, but what happened was an incredible thing for me.'

Since then, Paul has only had two serious relationships — both at university where he was studying computer-aided design. The first was with a blonde called Melanie. That fizzled out after less than a year. The second, with a brunette called Phillipa, was more serious. They parted around the millennium.

Paul said, 'I met Melanie within two weeks of starting my course. She was fun and attractive. She was on a hotel management course and I fell for her the first time I saw her. It was quite a happy relationship but not always easy because we were both quite serious about our studies. We were together for eight months which is the longest I'd been with someone. Towards the end, though, we drifted apart. When we did break up, all my friends told me that they weren't too shocked. They didn't think we were right together.

'I stayed single for about a year after Melanie and then along came Phillipa. I was well in love with her. She was really bubbly and incredibly good-looking. She really held herself together and people were impressed when they met her. Best of all, she loved to travel. We had some great holidays together. I really can't say a bad word about her.

'She was intelligent and she had this great aura. We even talked about engagement and marriage, but I think deep down we knew it was never going to happen. After she finished her studies, she wanted to move to London and I'm afraid I didn't. I enjoyed living with my parents in Reading and being with my mates.

'But maybe there was more to the end of the relationship than that. She was still at unversity through most of our dating and I'd started work. I was travelling like mad as well, and it just got too much. We'd planned this fantastic holiday together in Mexico to see in the millennium. We spent thousands, but she told me it was all over at my work's Christmas party. She really broke me. I was gutted. There wasn't anyone else involved. After a few weeks, I knew I had to move on. I had to get over this.'

Describing his dream woman, Paul said, 'I like girlie girls. Girls who are bubbly.' Girls like Helen Adams, in fact.

Paul added, 'And I'm a bit of a romantic. I love candlelit dinners and all that stuff. I love buying Christmas presents and springing surprises on girlfriends. I once secretly arranged for one to go horse-riding on Valentine's Day then whisked her off for a romantic meal.

'I often use the phrase "I love you". One Christmas, I made an advent calendar and put little presents behind every day leading up to the 25th. But I am a guy who wants a girl who's 50-50. For example, if I took a girl out on a date for dinner, I'd pay. But if after the third date she hadn't even offered to go halves or pay for the meal, she wouldn't be my type.'

Paul grew in confidence over his eight weeks in the *Big Brother* house, though he only escaped being nominated twice. At first, being so obviously rejected by his housemates had a terrible effect on his fragile ego. But then, as it dawned on him that the public liked him far more than the people he was cocooned with, he visibly picked up.

A key moment was the eviction vote at the end of the fifth week when he was up against Bubble. Everyone assumed that Paul would get the bullet but, miraculously, he won — largely because viewers were desperate to see his romance develop with Helen. After that, nothing could dent his self-esteem. Paul began to think that he was invincible and that he could actually win *Big Brother*.

Brian thought so, too — and tipped him to pick up the £70,000 first prize, despite making no secret of the fact that he loathed him. But after surviving four nominations, Paul was easily beaten by his TV girlfriend Helen when they were up against each other in the penultimate week.

Paul said that he got on least well with Amma in the house. 'We got off to a bad start but I'll give the girl a break and see where it goes,' he said. 'I also disliked Bubble but he gained my respect when he left because he spoke the truth.'

Paul also kept the other house-mates awake with his sleep-talking. One night, he even gave his acceptance speech, imagining he'd won the show. 'I'd like to congratulate everyone for voting for me,' he said.

Certainly, his family supported him week in, week out. Mum Jenny, 50, her Hollywood set designer husband Ken, 51, their graphic designer daughter Nicky, 23, and younger son Lee, 14, were all hurt that Paul was branded 'boring' by his housemates.

Jenny told the *Mirror*, 'It really annoyed me, becuase he wasn't showing off or playing to the cameras like the other people in the house. Paul is not boring. He's a down-to-earth lad who likes women, drinks and parties and not worrying about tomorrow. He had friends coming from as far as Italy and Denmark when he was nominated and I don't think they'd have done that for someone who was dull.'

As well as romancing Helen, Paul now hopes to pursue a career in showbusiness. He impressed bosses at Virgin Radio when he DJ'ed in their lunchtime slot for two hours after his eviction, and with his clean-cut good looks, he is being lined up for TV presenter roles. So far, though, there have been no concrete deals.

But who knows — maybe he'll get a starring role in *Big Brother*'s first wedding.

CHAPTER 9

VOLVO SEX & SLIPPERY LEGS IN A HOT TUB – ELIZABETH WOODCOCK

'We keep slipping off each other. It's all legs,
and then your boobs start poking out.
Feel the water and how oily it is.
Would you like to jump in here?'
ELIZABETH WOODCOCK

Sliding nude across the seats of a Volvo estate, the well-worn leather moulding to her pert buttocks, Elizabeth Woodcock was the pulsating image of a willing sex kitten. It was an image that screamed 'The back seats fold flat, so there's plenty of room for absolutely anything. I could even jam my feet against the seatbelts.'

Behind the camera was her boyfriend Stephen Druitt. And, as she watched the long camera lens explore every inch of her nakedness, 27-year-old Elizabeth moistened her lips in anticipation.

In another shot, she was pictured with her tongue poking out, Bubble-style, with two fingers over her nipples. In others she was naked with just the ticklish tassels of a scarf covering her boobs.

But what is most remarkable is that her boyfriend Stephen was no jack-the-lad. He is a 53-year-old, highly-respectable millionaire member of Edinburgh's rather snooty middle-class élite. A stalwart of the local sailing club, he is well spoken and lives in a sprawling £600,000 home in one the Scottish capital's most exclusive districts. In short, he's the last person you'd expect to be going out with a *Big Brother* contestant, let alone someone eager to tell all about their exotic, exhausting sex life.

But that's exactly what he did, and Stephen became easily the highest-profile partner of any of the contestants. While most shunned the limelight, widower Stephen never missed an opportunity to talk up his girlfriend. It seemed as though he were running a campaign to boost her chances of winning *Big Brother* from outside the house. And the key to this campaign were those pictures, snapped on a romantic holiday together before she entered the *Big Brother* house.

Stephen was also happy to detail exactly what they did when Elizabeth was naked. His message was clear — my Liz may come over as a frump on the telly, but in reality she's a little minx. Vote for Liz.

Describing one particularly memorable encounter they enjoyed on a remote beach in Chile, he talked about sea and sand swirling over their naked bodies and said, 'For 364 days of the year there's a low tide on this beach — the night we stayed was the one night with a high tide.

'We stripped off inside our little tent and began making love in the soft sands. Suddenly, I could feel water lapping against my feet as the waves crashed against the tent. In no time, the tent was full of water and we were soaked.'

There was sex, too, in that red Volvo estate. 'Sometimes the mood just overtakes you,' he said. 'We stripped off and did it in the back. Other times we've had sex in the Scottish mountains, but the midges and the cold make outdoor sex there very difficult.'

No such problems at an Italian villa, though. 'We got up from bed, put on our dressing gowns and wandered outside,' he recalled. 'We stripped naked, caressed and then had sex to the sound of the crickets around us. Elizabeth's a wonderful lover. To me she's like a scaled-down Marilyn Monroe. And like any woman, she enjoys a lot of attention in bed. She doesn't want it all to be over in ten minutes.'

Elizabeth revealed that Stephen was her first proper boyfriend, though she'd had several lovers before him. They met when she began temping for his Edinburgh-based travel consultancy and were friends for months before he sent her a Valentine's card. Soon after that, they became lovers, and the age gap had never bothered her.

'People are people,' she told the *Daily Mail*. 'Age is irrelevant. He's a person as far as I am concerned. People have asked me what I'd do ten years down the line when he was almost 70 and I wanted to have children,' she added. 'But I could be with someone at 25 who had a heart defect or got run over by a bus.'

Nevertheless, her parents didn't take too kindly when their daughter revealed she was moving in with him. Still, all that changed when they met him. 'They had so much in common and were getting on like a house on fire talking about the war,' she said.

Elizabeth, from Cumbria, blatantly used sex to beat 50,000 other applicants to a place on *Big Brother*. She had been on the final shortlist to appear in the first series and spent an anxious few weeks hoping to be drafted in as a last-minute replacement, but the call never came.

She had no hesitation in trying again for the second series and impressed producers with a remarkable home-made 'strip' video — filmed, of course, by the ever-eager Stephen.

The show's bosses, desperate to increase the sex content of the show, were so impressed with the sequence that they set it as a benchmark for other applicants.

Stephen explained, 'It was entirely her idea and it certainly seemed to work.'

The video was filmed at 5.30am on cold and blustery Gullane beach in East Lothian. 'We did it three mornings in a row until she was happy with it,' said Stephen. 'It's the only time I've ever used the camcorder.'

The sequence opens with Elizabeth — Betty to her pals in the TV house — facing the camera in clothing appropriate for a chilly morning on an out-of-season beach. Beside her stands a small table with a loaf of fresh bread (baking is one of her favourite pastimes) and a bottle of The Macallan

JULES STENSON & LEWIS PANTHER

whisky, her tipple of choice. After briefly introducing herself, she launches into her life story, using each item of clothing as a signpost for an aspect of her personality or a memorable experience.

As each tale is told, the relevant garment is removed and flung behind her into the wind. Finally, she is left shivering in a pair of black thermal knickers and a red bikini top. The knickers, she says, were a godsend during a trip to Patagonia where she went white-water rafting with her brother.

Then the knickers go, too, though the camera does not lower its focus and her modesty is protected. The final item, the bikini top, was chosen by a man with whom she fell in love during a year in Spain. She sighs as she recalls that he turned out to be homosexual.

With that the top comes off and Elizabeth runs naked into the sea, providing the camera with a full-length back view.

Channel 4 chiefs must have been hoping for more of the same when the exhibitionist joined the other TV housemates. But Elizabeth turned out to be a profound disappointment. With one notable exception, she kept her clothes very much on, and always seemed to wear the same mauve fluffy jumper.

Elizabeth turned out to be the contestant the other housemates loved — and whom the public hated. The mousey web designer was regularly booed by the crowds waiting outside the *Big Brother* house when her name was mentioned by Davina McCall. She was dismissed as scheming, two-faced and, above all, boring.

No one outside the house — apart

from Stephen — had a good word to say about her and she was considered a certainty to be booted out of the house as soon as she was nominated.

But, in the end, Elizabeth was never nominated. She barely even attracted a nomination vote. The other housemates found her indispensable. Time and again they came up with the same phrases to describe the posh Durham University politics graduate — 'the mother of the house', 'so kind and caring', 'always there with a shoulder to cry on'.

And there was her cooking, too. Elizabeth kept everyone fed night and day for 64 long days, happily passing on her skills to her new pals, most of whom could barely boil an egg.

Her great Interesting Moment came when she frolicked naked in the hot-tub with Amma and almost ended up in bed with her.

'I knew I would be criticised for being guarded and boring in the house, but you have to think about self-preservation,' she explained after being evicted. 'I was hardly going to lay myself bare to all these strangers. That would have been like an invitation for them all to stab me.'

And she admitted she'd have struggled to survive inside the house without her 'rock' — housemate Dean O'Loughlin.

Of all the contestants, Elizabeth was most critical of the show itself. She even questioned the decision to select Penny Ellis, the first housemate to be evicted, to take part. 'She was too fragile to cope,' she told the *Daily Mail*. 'I've been criticised for being guarded, but Penny was the exact opposite. She went crazy in there and when she was nominated, it destroyed her.'

Elizabeth also queried the way the show was edited, claiming she had been unfairly portrayed as 'patronising' on the daily *Big Brother* highlights. 'I know I was criticised for patronising Helen when I told her how to spell the word 'garlic' but I don't think people realise she is dyslexic,' explained Elizabeth. 'I didn't agree with Dean when he talked about having to 'intellectually downshift' because the others in the house weren't very clever. I thought that was going a bit far. Dean was my rock in the house. And no, there was nothing sexual going on between us, contrary to all the rumours.'

It had become a *Big Brother* tradition to make a fuss of birthdays, so the group serenaded Elizabeth on the stroke of midnight as she turned 27. She then had some surprise decision-making to do when *Big*

Brother gave her a choice of presents. Her options were the use of a running machine for one week, the ultimate pampering party for 50 minutes, or an evening spent in five-star bliss.

She took the party — and it turned out to be the raunchiest night in the history of *Big Brother* as Helen, Elizabeth and Amma stripped off in the hot-tub. The three girls took full advantage of the evening's hot water supply, as they sipped champagne and massaged each other under the soapy suds.

And it wasn't long before the boys wanted to get in on the action. Brian and Josh, however, were the only male housemates to be allowed in — at first! The boys quickly embarked on a drunken conversation concerning why gay men are allowed to see their female friends naked and heterosexuals aren't.

Paul took exception to the fact Brian and Josh were granted the liberty to be more 'touchy, feely' with girls simply because of their sexuality. Having quaffed a fair amount of Champagne, the girls finally decided that Paul shouldn't be left out and invited him to join them in the bathroom.

'I'm only doing this because I want to be one of the luckiest blokes in the country,' he grinned.

Elizabeth purred provocatively, 'We keep slipping off each other. It's all legs, and then your boobs start poking out. Feel the water and how oily it is. Would you like to jump in here?'

But the evening finally fizzled out with none of the contestants having sex.

And though it had been a great night, in the final few weeks Elizabeth began to sense that the public found her boring.

Nevertheless, she divided the house up into two groups. The 'Sensibles' — her, Dean and Josh. And the 'Exciting' group — Helen, Brian and Bubble.

Elizabeth finally came fourth in *Big Brother*, leaving on the penultimate day of the show when Channel 4 bosses introduced a surprise eviction. Of the final four, she had attracted just 2 per cent of the votes.

She held her head and wept when told the news but, within a matter of seconds, she was jumping around at the thought of being reunited with her family. Sure enough, Stephen was outside waiting to greet her. Since leaving *Big Brother*, she has returned to Edinburgh to live with him.

'Hosting the Big Breakfast is the last thing I'd want to do,' she frowned. 'I fancy going to Mongolia soon. But first I need to readjust to living in the real world. That might take a little while.'

CHAPTER 10

NAKED URGES & A SECRET POTION IN THE NIGHT – DEAN O'LOUGHLIN

'In the end, you just have to find a
discreet way of relieving the tension –
and, believe me, when you know there
are cameras on you, that's not easy!'

DEAN O'LOUGHLIN

The longing would come first, then the dull ache. Alone in his *Big Brother* bed, Dean O'Loughlin couldn't stop fantasising about his air stewardess fiancée Vanessa Jones. He'd imagine the stunning 31-year-old spreadeagled naked, waiting only for him. Dean's suppressed urges got so uncomfortable that he slurped a special 'anti-sex' potion to calm him down.

'I was really worried how I'd cope without sex for nine weeks,' he told the *Sunday People*. 'I take herbal medicine for my digestion and when I saw my herbalist a few weeks before going in, he suggested adding some different ingredients to chill me out and calm my libido down. I took it every day but I think I really needed a double dose. By Week 5 it was getting hard — I missed sex so much.

'All the guys found it really difficult, and some of the girls, too. In the end, you just have to find a discreet way of relieving the tension — and, believe me, when you know there are cameras on you, that's not easy!

'I'd picture Vanessa at home, doing normal things like cooking. Of course, there were other times when I thought about her differently — particularly naked! And when Amma, Elizabeth and Helen were in that hot tub, I just had to keep out of it completely. I knew Vanessa would be tuning in at that point.

'I can honestly say that finally leaving the house was an incredible relief — in all senses. And being reunited with Vanessa was just mind-blowing. We stayed the night at a lovely hotel and talked and made love until 5am. After so long I thought it would be an instant physical thing. But it was so emotional — lots and lots of love and feelings.'

Dean, 37, was dubbed *Big Brother*'s Big Daddy because, as the oldest housemate, he'd certainly lived a fair bit before he strolled into the confines of the television compound, guitar in hand.

With his broad Black Country accent, he dished out pearls of wisdom throughout his 64-day stay and made sure he had enough pairs of underpants to last a fortnight at a time!

He even dared to question some of the rules imposed by the faceless voice of Big Brother. This earned him the respect of the others and helped him avoid a nomination for eviction before the very last programme.

But the shaven-headed internet businessman was no angel before — and even during — the Channel 4 show. He openly and grumpily admitted hating the 'daddy' role he had unwittingly taken up, belittling his fellow contestants in the process with an angry broadside at his problem kids. But like a typically stressed-out father, he confessed, 'I ended up loving them to death ... they're wonderful. I'll care about them for ever.'

Brummie Dean was the voice of reason when the likes of Helen or Brian would ask if they could start on the day's quota of booze. 'I found myself saying, "Er, no, I think we'd better wait until later,"' moaned Dean. 'When we'd had a few drinks, they could become like a bunch of over-excited children. They'd drive you mad for a bit but because you loved them you weren't irritated for long.

'Sometimes, Helen would just explode in a ball of glitter and noise and sparkle and you'd want to say, "SIT DOWN!" But she was lovely. She was like my 12-year-old daughter, but later on she started showing real, level-headed maturity and I felt very proud of her.

'Brian would be running around the place at 2.00am when I was trying to get to sleep but because he had me in fits of laughter the whole time that was cool, too.

'When there was a lot of booze involved, it could get a bit wild. After

JULES STENSON & LEWIS PANTHER

a while, of course, I realised I was turning into the boring, sensible one. I fell into the Big Daddy role because I'm too old and too bald to be in a boy band and I come across as a responsible character. It was weird because it just came naturally. Helen would come up and ask my advice and I'd just give her a straight answer. Then Brian would ask me something and again I tried to be as honest and sensible as possible. But I sometimes got a bit cheesed off — what with Amma sometimes in tears in one corner and Penny in another.

'But I did try and rebel against the father figure thing a few times. And when I was dressing up in Narinder's clothes and prancing about in wigs, no one could have called me square. But after eight weeks of dressing up and doing playground games, I was starting to feel a bit bored. I also learned all I *ever* want to know about Destiny's Child, Posh and Becks, make-up and glitter. I was thinking, "Let me out! Let me talk politics and the state of the world!" But even so I felt proud that I'd got respect and affection from the other housemates. I still feel protective of Helen and Brian and think I will for a long time yet. I'd love it if they kept in touch with me and asked me for advice.'

Dean did have to fend off some unwanted attention from Elizabeth as the posh Cumbrian made play after play for him. But he insists he never noticed she was openly flirting with him.

'Maybe I was just being a stupid bloke but I really didn't see it,' he said. 'I bonded with Elizabeth because we could talk about serious issues, but there was never anything sexual.'

Now that marriage to Vanessa is in

the air, Dean is even contemplating having children of his own, especially after dealing so well with his 'problem kids'.

'I don't know whether we will have children, but my experience as Big Daddy has certainly given me something to think about in that department,' he smiled.

Dean's devotion to Vanessa showed through in his determination to get messages to her by wearing T-shirts displaying secret love codes. He also admitted wearing a special shirt designed by a pal with 'Gameford' written on it. 'I knew there'd be a time in here when things got a bit sticky and told her I would put that one on so they knew it was getting tough,' he said.

At the time, a *Big Brother* spokeswoman announced, 'Dean will be told he is not allowed to wear any of these shirts again.'

But despite his clear devotion to Vanessa, Dean admitted during a lazy chat with Elizabeth four weeks into the series that he was by no means Mr Perfect and had cheated on women more than once. He'd even dumped one girl because she was too nice!

During another of their early deck-chair chats, Dean and Elizabeth discussed their experiences of adultery.

Dean admitted that he had 'overlapped' in the past, glossing over his two-timing. But he went on to tell Elizabeth how he started seeing a woman in Birmingham when his then-girlfriend moved to Brighton.

The strain of leading a double life proved too much for Dean, who slipped up by asking the Brighton girl about the Birmingham girl's brother. He concluded that women were much better at affairs than men.

Elizabeth, however, had been on

the receiving end of adultery and wasn't as laid back about the subject.

Both agreed, though, that a one-night mistake and an organised, lengthy affair were very different things, although there were sometimes 'understandable circumstances'.

Mind you, dumping a young love and stealing your best mate's stripper girlfriend seems a bit tricky to stretch to 'understandable circumstances'.

Dean cheekily wooed beautiful American lap-dancer Kimberley Morgan from his best pal and left his childhood sweetheart Shirley Jones in the process. He told the *Mirror*, 'Dean met Kimberley when he came over to visit me in the States in 1992. She looked a bit like Joanne Whalley-Kilmer and Dean stole her off me. Then in 1993, she came to Britain and they met up again. They went out for about three years. While she was here, she worked at the Legs Eleven club as a stripper. Eventually, though, she went back to California. It was a good thing — she was a bit mad.'

He has forgiven his mate, with whom he has been through thick and thin over the past two decades. 'Dean doesn't shout and scream like the rest of the contestants in the house,' he said, 'but he's not boring, he's just not an attention-seeker.'

Nevertheless, under interrogation by Elizabeth and Stuart, Dean did display a wild side. And beneath that mild-mannered exterior beats the heart of a wannabe heart-throb! Elizabeth unwittingly provoked the revelation when she started discussing escort work.

The look on her face was one of complete surprise when he announced matter-of-factly that he had had interviews for escort work. He revealed he might have got hundreds for one night's work.

Mind you, that isn't the only skeleton to come clattering out of Dean's cupboard. His best pal revealed that Dean suffered psychological problems after taking too much Ecstasy on a trip to New York. He had given him the drug as the pair prepared to tour the city's hot spots.

'Dean doesn't do drugs,' he added. 'But he'd never been to New York before and got caught up in the moment. We were staying at my friend's apartment by Madison Square Gardens. I had a pile of Ecstasy in front of me and I was making it into tablets. I got the top off a Biro and scooped some up and gave it to him. Obviously, it was far too much. It sent him a bit mad.

'At first, he was really euphoric. We really ripped New York up for the night. Went round everywhere. But then he started having panic attacks and thinking the building he was in was about to collapse. The feelings kept returning for about six months afterwards. I felt really, really bad because I'd handed him the stuff and it gave him real mental problems.'

The psychiatric problems, panic attacks and paranoia made Dean determined never to touch Ecstasy again. He said he thought he was going to die. His personality had changed since though. He stopped being quite so arrogant.

Dean nearly slipped up a month into the *Big Brother* series when he gave his guitar a rest and started experimenting with fruit, making a cigarette from banana skins.

As he was about to light the fruity roll-up on Day 28, *Big Brother* called him to the Diary Room to advise him not to smoke it because of 'health implications'.

Dean wasn't happy. 'Why did they watch me make the thing? It's not illegal,' he argued.

Dean, whose dad died of a diabetes-related disease, grew up as one of six children in a tough part of Birmingham. 'Our rooms were freezing,' Dean told the group of housemates in the first fortnight of the show. 'You'd go to shut your curtains and they'd be frozen to the window.' Compared to that, he said, taking part in *Big Brother* was a doddle, and added, 'I went to bed hungry so many times.'

Elizabeth was horrified. She said how lucky she was – they even had electric blankets as children!

That upbringing has led Dean to become involved in volunteer projects in his home town. Along with the

Birmingham Youth Clubs Association, he set up a recording studio running voluntary sessions for rebellious youngsters.

Dean's mum Sheila, 70, helped him build the place, climbing ladders while clutching a hammer and nails.

He first considered entering *Big Brother* when he and Micky were watching last year's contest. Micky revealed, 'He was saying, "I could do that." He's patient and he doesn't react. People can piss him off but he doesn't show it.

'Narinder was trying to get everyone to gang up on him over his guitar-playing, but he wouldn't be spiteful or angry. He'd have just said to himself, "OK, if that's the sort of person you are, then I'm not going to bother with you."

'He didn't put any falseness into it and he didn't make any attempt to be over-friendly with anybody. Dean's been described as boring, by Narinder's husband among others, but he's not. He's been a musician since he was 14 and on stage all his life. He's not really interested in all that. He's interested in the experience, being locked away with strangers for ten weeks.'

The experience did finally wear a bit thin, though, when he got fed up for a while and branded the other housemates a bunch of thickheads. He moaned that he couldn't stand their 'boring and stupid' conversations and claimed he had to 'intellectually downshift' to fit in.

His remarks were made as lap-dancer Amma and designer Paul prepared to go head to head in a battle to avoid being evicted.

Still, he did manage to focus on some of the smaller things in life. With just 14 days to the end of *Big Brother*, Dean had a triumphant smile on his face as he revealed he had just enough clean pants to last to the end!.

Then he returned to strumming his guitar, revelling in his memories of being a singer-songwriter with a band called L Kage. The four-piece made just one album, called *Brazilliant*, in 1993. It sounded like a cross between the Happy Mondays and REM. Though they were dropped by their record company soon after, the determination Dean showed in getting the deal in the first place came to his aid again. This time, though, it helped him into the *Guinness Book of Records*.

On Day 34 in the house, he made the world's biggest tower of sugar cubes, smashing the previous record by 18cm!

An official Guinness World Record adjudicator confirmed that Dean's sugar tower stood at 1m 20.1cm. He had completed it in two hours.

Dean's achievement easily trumped other housemates' record attempts at sweetcorn-munching, cream cracker-scoffing and bubblegum-blowing. As Helen excitedly chanted 'Dean is the main man!'

CHAPTER 11

LOVE, LAUGHTER & A BOYFRIEND GETS THE CHOP – HELEN ADAMS

*'Just because I'm blonde and
OK-looking, people think I'm dumb ...
It's OK – I live in Helen's world.'*
HELEN ADAMS

She is unquestionably a star, but her first step into the *Big Brother* house was a testimony to Helen Adams' sheer guts and determination.

Throughout her life, she has had to battle dyslexia to learn to read and write. She needed her mother's help to fill in the 14-page application form, yet beat off 50,000 other applicants. And once she was in the house, there was no doubting that the producers had made the right choice. She was brilliant.

Mum Liz, a nursery nurse, said, 'I'm very proud of Helen. It's been her biggest battle in her life. She's always tried to hide it and hasn't told any of her boyfriends before.'

Helen thought there was a 'K' in 'garlic'. And because of her problems with word-confusion, she could never pronounce *Big Brother* contestant Narinder's name properly. Helen would call her Navinder by mistake. Narinder thought she was being rude — she wasn't. She simply could not get her head around such a new and long word.

When the subject of dyslexia was raised in the *Big Brother* house in an early-hours conversation, Helen made only a passing reference to her condition. But she got her bank account numbers mixed up, which meant that expenses from the series, paid to make up for lost earnings, failed to get to her. And if she'd won the £70,000 first prize, Helen pledged to give £10,000 to the British Dyslexia Association to help other sufferers.

Helen took in *Bridget Jones's Diary* to the *Big Brother* house because it is well laid-out and easy to read. 'And she's seen the film so that helps,' added Liz. 'In fact, Helen just has to work twice as hard as anybody else to get by.'

This might surprise fans of *Big Brother*, who may have assumed that Helen was nothing more than the original 'dumb blonde'. They could all be forgiven though, as the fluffy hairdresser — who wondered whether there really was chicken in chick peas — played up to every preconception that there is about blondes being dumb.

The chick pea gaffe was one of many daft comments she came up with in the house, the most famous of which — 'I love blinking, I do' — has even become a national catchphrase.

Her other catchphrase was her declaration of surprise and joy — 'Ohhhh … myyyyy … God.'

The Welsh beauty explained all this zaniness by saying simply, 'It's OK — I live in Helen's world.' And Helen's world, in all its confusions, was really like no other.

Helen also showed quite astonishing naïveté and ignorance. She may well have been fiercely proud of her Welsh roots, but not enough to know that Cardiff was the capital of the principality.

She once lamented, 'Just because I'm blonde and OK-looking, people think I'm dumb.'

Lovable Helen came up with plenty of other reasons for viewers to come to that conclusion. For instance, it took her four weeks in the *Big Brother* house to conclude that she was the only Welsh person there.

She was aware that it was obvious to all viewers exactly where she came from.

Helen could say the oddest things about almost any subject. Tucking into one of Elizabeth's delicious dinners one night, she looked up and with a crammed full mouth said how amazing it was she could get it all in!

On the subject of food again, she declared that she was 'the Porridge Princess'. She was so proud of her porridge recipe she even detailed it in an article in the *Sun* after leaving the *Big Brother* house.

It wasn't just chick peas which left Helen confused. She also asked, 'What's in kidney beans?' Presumably kidneys, in Helen's World.

And although she happily

munched into chicken, she wasn't sure about eating the male species of the bird. In a hilarious, fowled-mouthed slip, she once asked, 'You know those chickens out there? Can you eat cock?' And no, she wasn't talking about Paul Clarke or Big G.

As the other housemates struggled to stop collapsing into fits of giggles,she tried to explain herself.

Helen was clearly no culinary genius, and had no idea how jelly was made. She once asked if the jelly was cooked!

Politics was definitely not her strong point. To be fair to her, gay winner Brian wasn't much of a political animal, either.

He once argued that there should only be one political party controlling us all, until the more astute Dean pointed that might be problem if they decided to ban homosexuality.

Helen was anxious not to alienate any viewers who may want to vote for her by expressing any strident political opinions. She once asked what the Liberal democrats stood for.

Helen left school with two GCSEs — one in art and the other, remarkably given her dyslexia, in English. She failed to appreciate that other people may have taken more than just the two exams. She also seemed to have difficulty understanding the rules of *Big Brother* — failing to appreciate that each week one of the contestants is voted out. She appeared particularly puzzled after Stuart was evicted, saying that it didn't seem that there was as many of them as at the start.

Music wasn't a strong point, either. As Dean strummed away at the Burt Bacharach classic ballad, 'The Look of Love', she asked him if it was one of his songs.

She was wary of Big Brother and the cameras around the house, although for the first few weeks she thought there were only two cameras.

It was the infra-red night cameras which particularly worried her, as she believed they could see under the duvet covers.

This wasn't James Bond, though — Helen and Paul were able to maintain some privacy hidden by their orange quilts.

Helen thought that her and Paul could escape Big Brother's gaze in various spots in the house. As they were in the kitchen one night, she told him, 'There are no cameras on us here.'

He replied, 'Except for the big one behind the mirror staring right at us.'

There were plenty of gaps in her celebrity knowledge, too. She once asked if Jack Daniels was the guy who does all the magic stuff.

Sex often left her confused. Josh said one morning that he had had four wet dreams, and woke up in the morning covered. Helen asked him, 'Covered in what?'

While playing the alphabet game, Helen had to name an animal beginning with 'A'. She said, 'Bee.'

When it got to 'F', she shouted, 'Frankfurt'; for 'I' — 'Igloo'; and for 'O' — 'Origami'. Helen also was confused on the letter 'J'. With a proud grin, she said, 'Jimmy.'

Dean asked, 'What's that?'

Helen replied, 'A baby kangaroo, of course.' She meant a joey.

Helen's catchphrases became so cool that T-shirts were made featuring the most popular ones. The one everyone wanted had her most famous one on it — 'I love blinking, I do.'

The £12 T-shirts were designed by Nigel Harrison at The Dragon Shop in Cardiff. 'They have gone like hot cakes,' he said. 'I came up with the idea because Helen's phrases are catchy and fun and I realised that the Welsh really do speak backwards sometimes.'

Helen may have found many things bewildering, but she had a clear idea about what she looked for in a man and soon, after entering the TV house, she secretly concluded that her relationship with Gavin 'Big G' Cox had no future.

Liz also revealed the truth about her relationship with Big G, the boyfriend she effectively dumped while she was making eyes at Paul Clarke in the TV house.

'I never really got to know him that well because he was always distant and aloof and didn't seem to want to mix with us,' she said. 'Helen didn't see him that much because she was always at her dance classes. All Helen's boyfriends had to fit around her dancing. She'd go to work at the hairdresser's, then on to a dance class until eight or nine o'clock at night and then maybe once a week she'd drive down to Cardiff to see him.

'He wasn't that touchy-feely or romantic with Helen when we did see them, either. I can't remember seeing him put his arm round her on the odd occasion when he came to dinner. And there was no talk of engagements. In fact, he didn't do that much talking at all. Just recently, while Helen was on *Big Brother*, he laid a patio for me which was really nice, I can't criticise him for that. But when some friends came round while he was there, he got up and carried on working and ignored us. It was very strange.

'We were all a bit flabbergasted when Gavin claimed he'd planned to propose to Helen when she came out. It's just him being over-dramatic. In fact, I was a bit shocked when Helen kept going on about Big G during the first few weeks that she was in the house. I hadn't thought it was that serious.

'Helen had been through a rough patch with him and told her friends that they might be on the verge of splitting up a few weeks before she went on to *Big Brother*. I'd had a few funny phone calls from Helen over the fact that things between her and Gavin weren't right, but she wouldn't confide in us about him if things weren't going well.

'So for Gavin to go on about marriage was a bit rich. When we used to tease Helen about settling down with kids, she'd laugh and poo-

poo the idea saying, "There's not much chance of that."

'We'd ask when she was moving in with him and he'd say, 'Ooooh, leave it out, I'm not having none of that, I know which side my bread is buttered."

'I thought of it as a very casual relationship before Helen went on to *Big Brother*. I think what has happened is that he let her do all the chasing and when he realised he wasn't getting all his own way, he didn't like it.'

After viewers saw Helen and Paul Clarke smooching under a blanket, Gavin phoned Liz, demanding to know if she'd seen the show.

Liz said, 'He was ranting on, "Well, it looks as if you're going to get a son-in-law from Reading." He was really over the top.

'I said to him, "Look, Gavin. It's

only a game show and they've not done anything apart from flirt." I told him that they'd not even kissed properly and that it was really surreal on that programme.

'Rhoda, Helen's best friend, had to speak to him on the phone for an hour to try to cheer him up but it didn't work. At one stage, he threatened to leave the country.'

Birmingham-born Gavin, 30, met hairdresser Helen on a blind date organised by her boss. But he didn't want her to go on to *Big Brother*, said Liz.

'Helen was too scared to tell him at first, until she had gone too far down the line to back out,' she added. 'We'd ask her if she'd told him and she'd just shrug her shoulders and say, "Not yet." She'd been to the first interview to get on *Big Brother* before she told him. And when he did find out he kept saying, "I can't believe she's applied for that thing."

'When Helen first introduced me to him he seemed like a nice bloke, but I always thought he was a bit too serious for her and a bit too old. They're not a good match.'

As she watched from the sidelines, making the 300-mile round trip from South Wales to East London, Liz became thrilled by her daughter's blossoming relationship with Paul.

'Who knows if they'll become involved in a serious relationship,' she said early on. 'There's obviously something more than just friendship between Paul and Helen, there's a chemistry between them. You only have to look at the way their eyes follow each other around the room. I knew there was something more between them when Paul sat through the night with Helen while she was drunk, listening to her go on about all her troubles. He was nicer to her than anyone else on the programme.

'At first I thought she was flirting, but now it's something more than that. You've got to look at it realistically. If you've been thrown together and spent seven weeks in close company, something is going to happen. I've only seen Paul on TV, but I can quite honestly say that I feel more comfortable with him than Gavin.

'It's difficult, but I'd rather see Helen with him than Gavin. We'll certainly be inviting him down for dinner in the near future. I've never seen her act like she does with Paul. Not even with Gavin. Especially with Gavin, come to think of it.'

Meanwhile, the war of words was hotting up. Magnetics engineer Gavin said of Paul, 'He's said that he'll hit me if I thump him, but I'm not going to get involved in a fight with him. People might want that but I'm far too intelligent to do that. If that's his simplistic attitude, that's up to him. I'm not going to get in a slugfest over somebody I don't know, because that's not me. If he wants to be a stupid little boy, let him be that.'

Meanwhile, there were others keen to tell the world they knew Helen, too — such as 30-year-old Rory Kilgannon who said he had taken her virginity.

'Helen is very adventurous sexually,' he revealed. 'When we were together, she wanted it all the time, and she didn't care where.'

Rory first met Helen when he went for a haircut at the salon where she was working as an assistant in Newport, Gwent. 'I'd only gone in for a trim but we got chatting and we hit it off right away,' he said. 'Helen liked the fact I was an older man. I think she was attracted to me because I work out and try to keep in shape. She said she likes chunky men rather than slim men. And I think she liked the fact that I was an older man.

'She told me she'd never had sex with anyone before and it was three months before we finally got it together. I think she wanted to be sure about us first. But eventually it happened one afternoon at my place. Once we'd done it, there was no stopping her.

'It didn't matter where we were, she'd want it indoors or outdoors. Her old school was about three doors from where she lived and she liked doing it in the playground at night. I think she got a kick out of it, and it gave a new meaning to sex education.'

Red-haired Rory bought a new van for building work, but Helen quickly turned it into a passion wagon.

'She couldn't wait to get me in the back of it,' he sighed. 'She was mad for it — whatever chance she got, she would want it. She had respect for her parents because she was living with them and wouldn't do it there. But anywhere else she was very keen.

'It was pretty standard stuff. She wasn't into anything particularly kinky but she had quite an appetite for it. It was very exciting and she would have all these ideas about how to do it. We went on holiday to Corfu and we bought a pack of sex cards showing all different positions.

'She'd never been abroad before without her parents. We went through most of the hearts and the diamonds and then we ran out of time. It was just as well it rained a lot during that two weeks because we spent a lot of time in bed.'

It wasn't exactly gentlemanly to tell all, but Helen has had the last laugh. She is famous throughout the land, but just how many people have heard of Rory?

CHAPTER 12

GOODBYE TO GAY SECRETS, HELLO TO VICTORY – BRIAN DOWLING

*'I wouldn't say that I'm famous.
I'd just say I was a guy
who was lucky on a game show.'*
BRIAN DOWLING

Brilliant Brian Dowling was the runaway winner of *Big Brother*. People wondered if the public would take to a highly camp, gay, Irish air steward. But they did in their millions. Despite Channel 4's attempts to create a cliff-hanger by hyping runner-up Helen Adams's chances in the last week, Brian won at a canter. He was more than 1,500,000 votes ahead of Helen in the final vote.

The bookies knew he was a certainty for weeks and had made him the 5-1 on favourite when half the housemates were still in the TV house. But what was it about this 23-year-old from the tiny town of Rathangan in County Kildare, about 40 miles from Dublin, that made viewers love him so much.

King of the pranksters, Bubble, summed it up in one sentence. 'Brian, you're the funniest bloke I've ever met in my life,' he told the Ryanair 'trolley dolly'.

But it's not just humour that made Brian so lovable. There was a hint of danger to him; you never really knew what he was going to do next.

He won *Big Brother* in those crucial early weeks, when viewers don't really know the contestants and long for some action.

Soon, hordes of his supporters were descending on the *Big Brother* studios every Friday night for the eviction vote. Banners for Brian easily outnumbered those for the other contestants — and his supporters weren't all gay. He was a huge hit with young women, too.

Brian was always ready for the *craic*. He was, to use a term from the world of showbiz — a world he will now effortlessly embrace — 'box office'. Big box office.

More than any other contestant, he made *Big Brother II* more memorable than the first series and helped Channel 4 to see off the early threat they faced from ITV's own reality show — the much more lavishly funded *Survivor*, the endurance game centred on a jungle island in the South China Sea. While *Survivor* bombed in the ratings and attracted little interest from all-important tabloids, Brian made *Big Brother* cool and addictive.

Trend-setting magazines such as *Heat*, Brian's favourite, were very quick to pick up on his popularity. Clever and quick-witted, he also hit it off with the other contestants in the *Big Brother* house. One reason was because he was fantastic at diffusing potentially awkward situations. He could say the most outrageous things and no one would bat an eyelid. He jokingly called Penny Ellis 'a psycho' and 'a filthy whore'. Narinder was a 'a bitch' and Bubble 'common'. Paul was 'Duh-man, raised by Dopey the Dwarf'.

If the horribly uncool Stuart had said the same things he'd have been lynched. But Brian came out with them and everyone fell about laughing. And the viewers swooned. Now Brian is being dubbed 'the new Graham Norton' — another gay Irishman and TV natural. A brilliant future is predicted for him. He's expected to be the main presenter if *Big Brother* makers Endemol win the franchise for the *Big Breakfast* slot on Channel 4.

There has been similar heightened speculation about other *Big Brother* contestants, but none has really made it (winner Craig Phillips and pretty Melanie Hill have both enjoyed respectable TV careers since the first *Big Brother* without setting the world on fire).

For once, though, Brian may just live up to the hype. He proved this to many cynical media observers in the final press conference after winning *Big Brother*. The Irish media had been kicking up a storm over the fact that Brian's 17-year-old sister Tracey was pregnant 'by an older man' (in fact, he's a lad just a year older than her).

The furore had caused acute

embarrassment to Brian's parents Gerard, 41, Rosie, 40, and his five other sisters, all younger. It was the last subject on earth that Brian wanted to talk about after 64 days in the *Big Brother* house. But one particular Irish journalist wouldn't let go. He kept firing questions at Brian, and was keen to establish if his sister was aged 16 or 17.

Brian, showing the same uncanny ability to diffuse a tricky situation he had displayed brilliantly in the house, quipped, 'My sister is 56, she's having my child, it's all illegal, it's all evil, it's all dirty and it will all sell.' The whole room fell about laughing. Yes, we thought, Brian really is funny.

He has been performing in much the same way all his life. Brian was the classroom clown who could make the boys cry with laughter — yet his sensitive nature made him a confidant to the girls.

His devoted mum Rosie says he was a hit on *Big Brother* because he was just as he is in real life. 'Brian was just being himself,' she said. 'He's exactly the same as he always is. Brian loves people and he loves attention.'

Dad Gerry agreed, 'What you see on the TV is Brian. That's his personality.'

From the age of four, Brian, the eldest in a bustling and happy family of seven children, was a born entertainer who would act the fool for laughs. He was nicknamed Bambi at school because of his wide-eyed innocence and lovable personality. His dearest friend, Michelle Bagnall, 22, shared books with him at primary school and hairspray as teenagers. 'He's mad as a hatter,' she smiled. 'He was always messing, always had everyone laughing.'

But even as the teenager was fêted by his friends, teachers and family, he was in the midst of inner turmoil. He had known for some time that he was gay but feared he would break his parents' hearts if he confessed. The first person he confided in was Michelle, who recalls how liberated he felt once he'd 'come out'. But now he had to tell his family, and despite Michelle's assurances that they'd understand, Brian was petrified.

He told his sisters — Michelle, 22; Valerie, 20; Tracey, 17; Paula, 14; Aoife, 11; and Tara, 8 — and they all took it in their stride.

It was only weeks before the series started that Brian finally revealed the truth to his mum and dad. In the quiet Catholic village where he grew up, this was no small confession. He remembers every second ticking by after he told them. 'My mother looked at me sternly and said, "Now, Brian, are you trying to be fashionable?" Then she broke into a huge grin and said, "I'll love you however you choose to live your life," and gave me a big hug. My mother was prepared for how I'd behave on the show. I wasn't going to tone it down for anyone.'

Rosie says, 'My daughter Michelle told me first, it didn't come as a great surprise. Later, Brian sat down and said he was worried about how we'd react, but in the end it all became very jokey. Brian's dad has never had a problem with him being gay.'

Michelle Bagnall told the *Mirror*, 'People knew at school. He tried to hide it, but I don't think he was really completely aware himself until the final year.'

Brian went on holiday to Majorca, and finally came to terms with his sexuality when he enjoyed his first gay romance. He fell for footballer Marc Dixon, who wooed him with a love letter slipped inside an empty Evian bottle.

'We just went wild,' remembers the 28-year-old Arsenal reserve, who was working as a holiday rep. 'Lots of skinny-dipping and romantic meals together. Brian told me he'd never kissed a guy before.'

Michelle added, 'Going to Majorca changed Brian's life. We were 18, it was our first holiday abroad and I think the trip opened his eyes. He realised there was more to life and decided to come out to me there. It was the first time he'd actually said out loud that he was gay.

'I think being away made it easier — he felt more relaxed. We were sat on the beach one afternoon, and he just came out with it. I don't think he was nervous about telling me because he was sure about himself. It was great. I threw my arms around him. Another school friend, Suzanne, was with us so we went out and had a big celebration that night.

'Since then, he's introduced me to one boyfriend, but I thought he was a slimeball. He wasn't nice to Brian and the whole experience put him off relationships for a long, long time. He's had a few flings since, but nothing serious.'

Brian moved to England at 19 and worked for the budget airline Ryanair for three years before going on *Big Brother*. He settled into a rented house in Bishops Stortford, Hertfordshire, with pals from the airline.

During this time, a gay *EastEnders* star chatted him up on a flight and asked him out. Brian insisted, 'I'm not going to say who or I'll make a fool of myself.' He has kept his word and still refuses to name the star.

Despite living away from home, Brian had an incredibly sheltered life before going on the show. It was a naïve streak which endeared him to the nation. 'The first black person I've ever really had a conversation with was Amma,' he confessed. 'And the first Asian person I've connected with all my life was Narinder.'

He had never eaten a curry, either, and doused housemate Narinder's delicious Indian cuisine in ketchup. Far from feeling insulted, Narinder was charmed by his childlike innocence. She shared a steamy kiss with Brian and still nurses a soft spot for him.

'We were like sisters in the house, really,' she says. 'I don't know how I would have survived without him. He was my sanity in the house. He's so lovely, so unique.'

Brian revealed he was gay within an hour of entering the *Big Brother* house — but at first he only told the girls. The excitable Irishman answered Narinder's candid question about whether he was gay and admitted he was fearful of the other boys' reactions.

But Brian was not slow to pour out his problems to his housemates in the house. He even revealed a terrifying cancer scare when he was a teenager. 'When I was 18, I found this lump on my testicle,' he said. 'I really thought I was going to die. I was frightened to death.'

Fearing the worst, Brian went for a biopsy and waited with bated breath for the test results. 'All sorts of thoughts go through your mind,' he shuddered. When the news came through, he was ecstatic. 'I was given the all-clear — it was such a huge

JULES STENSON & LEWIS PANTHER

relief.'

Brian twice confessed that he wanted to leave the house — first as Narinder faced eviction. 'If she goes, I want to go. I don't want to be here any more. She's the only one that makes me laugh,' he lamented. Of course, he picked himself up, and then threatened to go again after Amma and Josh went. 'My priority is me,' he said firmly, 'and if I get pissed off with getting up every day and I find everyone is really annoying me, that's my fault, they're better off not having me around.

'I just want my life back. I've learnt things after eight weeks. I feel happy and confident to go. I've done my time and I'm happy with what I've done.'

Touchingly, he said it found it unbearable nominating people he liked — particularly Helen — as the game wore on. He became an agony aunt to the Cwmbran hairdresser in those final few days as she tried to work out how to cope with her feelings for housemate Paul.

Two housemates, Dean and Josh, made no secret of the fact that they separately craved sex in the house. For Dean, the problem was so bad that he took a herbal medicine to dull his urges.

Brian longed for sex, too. He even considered, albeit briefly, bedding one of the girls to sate his passion. 'Helen told me she was wondering if I really was gay,' he revealed. 'I told her, "So am I in here."'

He quelled his urges by exercising and found tiring games of volleyball the best remedy. He admitted, 'I remember thinking the first thing I'd be doing after getting out was putting that right.'

And so he did. Brian spent the night with a man called Keith straight after leaving the *Big Brother* house. They shared a room together at London's exclusive Charlotte Street Hotel. Keith is a dark-haired Scot in his mid-20s. They have been dating for a few months. But though Keith was at the TV studios with Brian's friends and family the night he won the show, it is a very stormy relationship. The pair have split several times.

And despite being gay, Brian is determined to father a child of his own one day. 'I do sometimes wish I was straight,' he sighed. 'Once you choose a gay life, you choose a lonely life and I do sometimes worry that I'll never be able to have children.'

Considering the problem for a while, he added firmly, 'Whatever happens, one day I'm going to be a father. I've never slept with a woman before, but I could. And if I could change anything, I'd like to be straight, have a girlfriend and get engaged.'

Brian also admitted that he was a spoilt brat as a child and could still be a 'selfish bastard' who flys off the handle because he was unable to see beyond his own image.

But, he insisted, it was childhood terror that led to his famous fear of the chickens in the *Big Brother* garden. He'd had a bad experience in the turkey pen!

That brought a belly laugh, though don't mention bellies to Brian because he was horrified at how much weight he'd put on in the TV house. A session with a tape measure revealed that in seven weeks his 32in waist had grown to 34in.

But if he was expecting sympathy

JULES STENSON & LEWIS PANTHER

from his housemates, he was looking in the wrong direction as they immediately set about taunting him with such phrases as 'Pork boy' and 'Lost as a child and raised by bakers!'

Unfortunately, he seemed genuinely upset by his newfound tubbiness.

But he could still retain a sense of fun about one part of his body — his head. Along with Josh, Brian had his bonce shaved to celebrate another week of escaping a nomination. Brian was first under the clippers.

Once the trauma was over, Brian admired his new look in the mirror. He thought he looked like a newborn baby.

His biggest regret was how he treated Josh, the other gay contestant. 'I hated him at times,' Brian said candidly. 'I also felt like shit over the way I treated him when we had an argument after he first came in the house. I didn't mean the things I said. I was really glad when Josh came in, it was great to have another gay man there.

'I was always very self-conscious around him. He dressed well and did have a lot of class. You could tell that he hangs out with the "in" crowd in London.'

Now Brian could easily be part of that crowd, but he appears genuinely surprised by his success on the show. 'I really don't know why I got all those votes,' he smiled. And brushing aside comparisons with Posh and Becks-style celebrity, he added straighforwardly, 'I wouldn't say that I'm famous. I'd just say I was a guy who was lucky on a game show.'

He was also amazed that the Irish people took an openly gay man to their hearts and supported him so strongly. 'I was very shocked about that,' he said. 'Being Irish, Catholic and gay was a big thing for me.'

In the immediate aftermath of his victory, he talked about returning to his £17,000-a-year job as a senior supervisor with Ryanair. 'I'll still be pushing my trolley down the aisle,' he said modestly. 'I plan to be back to work. I enjoy being an air steward, it's my job. I've been doing it for three-and-a-half years.'

But with TV executives dangling contracts in front of him, there was little chance of any return.

Brian has skipped the traditional showbiz route since leaving the house, largely avoiding media appearances and drinks at London's trendy Met Bar. He did make an effort for his loyal fans at the famous nightclub G-A-Y, turning up with *Big Brother* buddies Narinder, Penny and Amma. The crowd loved him, which was more than could be said for Penny (she reportedly had food thrown at her!) and Josh (who was booed off the stage some weeks ago).

Brian has been snapped up by agents Peter, Fraser and Dunlop who have masterminded the careers of stars such as Ewan McGregor and Dawn French. An announcement about his forthcoming TV career is imminent.

CHAPTER 13

SIGNIFICANT BIG BROTHER MOMENTS

Like any fly-on-the wall series, Big Brother II *had its low and high points. Days when little happened and days that were riveting TV.*

Here are some of the bits that we'll all remember most.

Day 1: The entry. Our first proper view of how the housemates will react to one another

Day 4: Viewers get an early first glimpse of *Big Brother* passion when blonde Penny enjoys a steamy snog with randy Paul. It is also reported that the blonde six-footer revealed to pals that she would be willing to have sex on screen for the £70,000 prize.

Day 5: Saucy schoolteacher Penny delights fans as she drops her towel and flashes her bits to the nation. School bosses warned they would sack her if she made love on camera.

Day 7: Flirty Penny dishes the dirt and revealed she spent a fortune on a boob job.

Day 8: Cheeky Bubble begs stripper Amma and Narinder for sex — but they both reject his advances.

Day 11: *Big Brother* fans are once more rewarded for their patience when embarrassed Narinder accidentally flashes her boobs and Penny shows off her entire body for the second time.

Day 12: Viewers are stunned to hear posh Liz confess to housemates that she has kissed a girl. Amma admits she also enjoys kissing women.

Day 13: Amma reveals she likes bedding men with shaven bits and music man Dean tells the group he is desperate to play with himself.

Day 14: Once again, Narinder bares all to the cameras and flashes her bottom.

Day 15: A busy day! Helen lets fans catch sight of her shapely rear in the shower room. Drama teacher Penny spends the whole afternoon trying to kiss Paul and cuddles him until the flustered lad snaps and pushes her off, muttering something about sexual harrassment. Penny is evicted after the nation votes to keep hunky Paul instead.

Day 16: The nation votes to replace the first evictee with property boss Josh who disappoints the girls when he reveals he's gay.

Day 18: Camp Brian slips into the Jacuzzi bubbles and manages to rip off Narinder's bikini.

Day 20: Viewers watch a steamy hot-tub romp as Brian licks and kisses the backs of hairdresser Helen and Narinder before jokily turning his attentions to Paul. Bubble brags he has bedded 100 women.

Day 21: Brian's birthday bash turns into a drink-fuelled battle ground. Brian and Josh argue in the hot tub and Stuart and Amma have a full-scale screaming match which leaves her in tears.

Day 22: Helen says she can't wait to leave the house so she can have hours of sex with lover Big G. Liz and Narinder show off their backsides. Stuart becomes the second evictee from the *Big Brother* house as thousands vote once more keep Paul inside.

Day 27: Helen finally allows viewers a glimpse of her breasts.

Day 29: The nation votes to boot out medical rep Narinder, again choosing to keep Paul in the game.

Day 35: Lucky viewers watch as Liz, Amma and Helen romp semi-naked in a hot soapy bath after celebrating Liz's birthday. Liz snogs Amma.

Day 36: Britain's men are once more treated to a display of Helen's charms as she emerges from the shower. Bubble is the fourth reject to leave the famous house. Yet again, the nation decided to keep Paul.

Day 39: Bubble poses in the papers with his girlfriend despite revelations that she played away while he was in the house.

Day 40: Yet again, Channel 4 fans are treated to flashes of flesh as Liz's nightie rides up and Amma drives the men wild in her G-string.

Day 41: Gay Josh admits he keeps having horny dreams.

Day 43: Helen enjoys a sneaky peek at Paul's naughty bits as he pops out of his shorts while they sit chatting. Amma leaves the house after Paul escapes eviction once more.

Day 44: Chirpy Bubble dumps girlfriend Stephanie for two-timing him.

Day 47: Sexual tension between Paul and Helen spirals as the flirty pair enjoy secret chats and longing glances.

Day 48: Helen's fella Big G tells how he has been driven mad with jealousy watching his girlfriend's antics in the house.

Day 49: Viewers catch a sight of Helen in a thong while she sneaks a peek at Paul's manhood as he sleeps. The pair enjoy a romantic meal and after-dinner cuddle in the den after the housemates successfully complete a dancing task.

Day 50: Big Brother addicts eagerly await passion between the courting couple as Josh is evicted.

Day 51: Unknown to Welsh wonder

Helen, her lover Big G dumps her because he is fed up with her flirting in the *BB* house. She begs Paul to spend the night in the den with her.

Day 52: Helen and Paul enjoy a saucy choc ice fight in the garden writhing and wriggling around the lawn.

Day 53: Desperate fans wait for some saucy action after Helen whispered to Paul that Big G was no longer her boyfriend.

Day 57: Randy Paul and sexy Helen battle it out on nominations day but the nation chooses to keep Helen in the house a while longer.

Day 58: Poor heartbroken Helen is left hugging and sniffing Paul's pillow after his eviction. She decides to snuggle in his bed.

Day 63: A surprise eviction vote results in Liz becoming the eighth person to leave the house. She only got 2 per cent of the vote out of the final four contestants.

Day 64: Dean comes third, leaving Helen and Brian to battle it out for the £70,000 first prize. In a dramatic finale, Helen comes second and a stunned Brian is declared this year's winner.

CHAPTER 14

LAST YEAR'S CONTESTANTS – AN UPDATE

Craig Phillips

The 29-year-old builder, who got a massive 3,539,683 votes to become *Big Brother*'s first British winner, endeared himself to the nation by giving away his £70,000 winnings to friend Joanne Harris so she could pay for the life-saving surgery she needed in the USA. Not surprisingly, he's the busiest of all, initially winning a five-album deal with Eternal Records, though that was later dropped.

He's been seen on TV doing a DIY programme called *Housecall*. Reflecting on his time in the house, he said, 'I missed the lack of responsibility. No keys, no credit cards. And all that time to think.'

Anna Nolan

The ex-trainee nun Anna, who came second in the competition which made her a gay icon, signed a television deal for more than £100,000 after appearing as co-host on Chris Evans's *TFI Friday*.

The 30-year-old from Dublin also had offers for her autobiography and has been involved in modelling work.

Darren Ramsay

The 23-year-old father of three reportedly picked up £100,000 promoting Chicken Tonight and was signed up by Select Models who see him as a TV presenter.

A former worker at the Millennium Dome, Darren, from South London, has so far fronted slots for The Disney Channel and Choice FM.

'It was four days after leaving the house that I realised my life had totally changed. People in the street were screaming, "There's Darren!"' he recalls. 'I don't regret doing *Big Brother*, although I didn't enjoy my time in the house.'

Nick Bateman

Nasty Nick, who was kicked out after trying to rig the vote, is living proof that scheming doesn't always work. Although he seemed to have a lucrative career after briefly becoming Britain's most hated man, his quest for fame has nose-dived. He picked up £70,000 to tell his story, but his book and video bombed, and his quiz show *Trust Me* never took off.

Despite being in talks to star in *EastEnders* and a Guy Ritchie film, the 33-year-old who charged £3,000 for public appearances was recently dropped by his agent.

Melanie Hill

The only contestant to be booed out of the house, Mel moaned that the show had typecast her as a 'sexy little babe'. But then she presented a *Big Brother*-style show called *Chained* on E4 which did see people having sex.

The 26-year-old former computer sales assistant was also a cover girl for *Marie Claire* for which she is also a travel writer. 'It was a real shock to come out of the house and find I'd been perceived as a flirt,' she says.

Claire Strutton

Florist Claire, who replaced Nasty Nick, just got time to flash her boobs and flirt with Craig before being voted out.

Now, after becoming an item with fellow contestant Thomas McDermott, she is expecting his baby.

Before becoming pregnant, the 25-year-old appeared in pantomime, appeared on a one-off Playtex bra ad and presented ITV's *Dance 2000*.

Tom McDermott

The former computer design consultant did some modelling and radio and TV work. In Northern Ireland, he worked as a roving reporter for *The Kelly Show*. He has been busy on the personal appearance circuit and has fronted company product launches.

Nichola Holt

After leaving the house, Nichola, originally an art teacher from Bolton, launched a bid to be a pop star. But her one and only single flopped.

Caroline O'Shea

The 37-year-old former sex aid saleswoman, who turned down £5,000 to model topless, is still keen to launch a career as a singer.

Caroline is probably most notable for her drunken rampage with housemate Nichola at a TV awards ceremony when she knocked Vanessa Feltz flying. After *Big Brother*, she admitted she was depressed. 'People think I'm a millionairess as I've been on TV and to a few showbiz parties,' she said. 'That couldn't be further from the truth.'

Andy Davidson

'Randy Andy', who was always trying to bed Melanie Hill on *Big Brother*, went back to his job as a cycle courier for a brief stint. After going travelling, he then he tried to break into TV presenting and radio work.

Sada Walkington

The first to be booted out, she published her relationship guide, *The Babe's Bible*, and is now planning a novel. Sales of her book were disappointing but the former model pocketed £25,000 for telling her story and £10,000 for promoting internet giant Yahoo.